4

A FOOTPATH IN
UMBRIA

LEARNING, LOVING AND LAUGHING IN ITALY

NANCY YUKTONIS SOLAK

Includes bibliographical references
   1. Umbria (Italy) - Description & travel. 2. Umbria (Italy) - Social life and customs.
   3. Solak, Nancy. 4. Solak, Nancy Yuktonis. 5. Americans - Italy - Umbria - Biography.
   I. Title.

Cover and interior design by Sara Reeside, Breathe Graphic Design

ISBN-10: ISBN 1-453-67944-8
ISBN-13: 9 78145 3 679449

Printed in the United States of America

TO RICH

FOREWORD

As a youngster it never occurred to me that some day I might travel to another country. Not only were foreign countries considered exotic to most children growing up in the 1950s, but the idea of actually visiting one was nearly unheard of, unless you were famous and wealthy like Audrey Hepburn and Grace Kelly.

For our twenty-fifth wedding anniversary, my husband Rich and I spent all of September in Europe. The moment we landed, and every day after that, I could not believe our good fortune.

After touring France, Austria, Switzerland, and Germany, Rich and I disembarked from a clean, fast, quiet train that had just crossed the Alps into Italy. We then boarded a "milk" train which departed with a diminutive "toot toot."

Gone were the varying shades of black, white and gray which constantly enveloped us from the ground and the sky north of the Alps. Now, in Italy, bright yellows and oranges dotted the landscape, the sky a pool of celestial blue, the earth variegated shades of greens and yellows. The warmth from the same sun that had only occasionally peeked out while north of the Alps, now sucked the dankness from my bones. As a born and bred "Nervous Nellie," I felt my shoulders relax. Up until this moment, I hadn't even realized they'd been tense.

The milk train, unlike the smoother ones up north, clickety-clacked, the sound clamoring through the windows which, to my delight, were open. As all the travelers' bodies jiggled in unison, the warm outside air blew in, whipping my hair every which way. Looking at the backs of the heads of other passengers, the wind played havoc with their hair too. Whenever the train bulleted into a tunnel, everyone's hair whooshed forward, parting it down the middle from the crowns of their heads to the clefts in their necks. As we sped through the darkness, an ever-increasing pressure built up in our ears. The clatter of metal wheels grating against metal track heightened, heightened and heightened until it hit an ear-splitting shrill, and then, the moment the train bolted into daylight, everyone's hair whooshed backward, the ear pressure vanished, the sound mellowed to a dull roar and the green of the treetops and bushes flashed by both sides of the train.

Outside the window, the tidy sparse yards we had become accustomed to seeing in Austria gave way to lush, sometimes overgrown gardens. Piles of detritus were stashed between outbuildings, leaned against fences and abandoned in the middle of fields.

At each stop, instead of people disembarking, more and more climbed aboard. Four adults could fit on two facing bench seats, with room for groceries and babies on their laps. People stood wide-legged in the aisle. Soon every square inch of the tiled floor hid from view.

I sat, knee to knee, across from an Italian gentleman, both of us careful not to touch, his legs spread out, mine held primly together between his. Neither of us so much as wiggled a toe throughout the trip. Not knowing where to set our gaze when the train sped through tunnels, we both closed our eyes, feigning the need to rest.

The racket of the train and the wind forced people to shout their conversations and, despite the noise, the language flowing from their mouths caressed my ears. Children chaotically stumbled to and from their seats, stepping on people's toes. Mothers shouted "*Basta! Basta!*" (Enough! Enough!)

For some inexplicable reason, I basked in the experience of this ride. Totally contrary to my genetic makeup, contrary to my usual behavior and preferences, contrary to all logic, I fell madly in love with Italy, its people and its chaos. I suspected I could learn something important from this country.

Four years after our first visit, we returned, this time with our grown children and Rich's mother and sister. This visit was as magical as the first. When it came time to leave, I, the ever-loving homebody, astounded myself. I asked Rich, "Wouldn't it be fun to live here?" He, being mad with wanderlust, didn't even blink before nodding.

We vowed, with as much gravitas as a wedding vow, to return for an extended period of time. We'd have to do it on a shoestring, but we'd do it one way or another.

What neither of us knew then was how this vow would challenge us: our habits, our upbringing and our outlook on life. Most surprising of all, though, was how the experience would challenge our relationship. ♥

1

READY, SET, GO

Whenever I tell someone I'm worried about something, the standard comeback is, "What's the worst that could happen?" Being of the nervous persuasion, the first thing that always comes to my mind is death. Relaxed people never seem to think of that.

Now, with the prospect of moving to another country, I've been pondering death more than usual. Since I believe in an afterlife, I try to calm my nerves by reasoning that moving and death are synonymous. Both are transitions from one place to another. A change of scene. A different point of view.

Two months from today, on January 11, my husband and I will depart our dearly beloved home in Michigan to live in Italy for at least a year. The expectation is clear — we're going to heaven!

Rich and I know how heavenly Italy can be in spring and fall. Perhaps January, particularly in the northern part of Umbria where we plan to settle, may not be as heavenly, but it will certainly constitute a transition, a change of venue.

The old saying, "You can't take it with you," is looking pretty good now as I stare at four seasons of clothes stacked around me in tippy piles, wondering what to bring, what to leave.

Friends say, "Buy them there." Sounds good, but this transition, unlike our final one, requires money. Though our lives are filled with abundance — family, friends and enough financial security to live comfortably, even live in a foreign country for awhile — there is a limit. Besides, we have to maintain our house in Michigan while we're gone. With the value of the U.S. dollar falling faster than sleet in December, buying new clothes sounds scandalous.

Whenever there's a transition at the library where I work, someone posts an announcement on the bulletin board. Once the sign went up about my leave of absence, one colleague after another rushed up to me. "Congratulations!" they'd say, followed immediately by, "Are you renting a villa?" Actually, no. We're renting an apartment. We will take public transportation and, whenever feasible, walk. My husband has no qualms about being a pack horse even if it means walking with both his luggage and some of mine. "Still," my co-workers say, "it sounds so romantic," and it does. If it's not romantic, then the adventure will be good for a laugh in our old age.

I feel duty-bound to explain that our preparations for this transition are nothing like the screenplay of Peter Mayle's nonfiction book-turned-movie, *A Year in Provence*. In the opening scene we see actors playing author Peter Mayle and his wife as they say goodbye to friends at what appears to be a retirement or bon voyage party in London. The next day their little blue car wends its way through the hills of Provence in France. They stop in front of a furnished villa they already own, carry a few suitcases inside, and start to live as though they'd only been away on vacation. No offense to Peter Mayle, but movies such as this are exactly what makes our journey sound so romantic to others. As if you party one night, go to bed, wake up, drive a couple hours and arrive in heaven. All of this is far easier, not to mention cheaper, for Europeans than for Americans who have to fly across an ocean to get to Italy.

We don't even see the Mayles jump through any hoops to obtain visas. For Americans, an extended visa (more than three months in Italy) takes planning and some bureaucratic aggravation. To prove we have enough money to support ourselves while there, for example, we have to open our financial records to strangers at the Italian Consulate in downtown Detroit for their review and judgment. The Consulate also needs proof that we have a place to live.

Our search for rentals began on the Internet and in travel magazine ads. Everything was expensive – between $400 and $1,000 per *week*. On the rare occasion when we found something reasonably priced, we couldn't determine what its surroundings looked like or its proximity to markets and city life. The location of our residence was too important to leave to chance. This was, after all, a dream – a costly dream. To fulfill it we had to secure a location that looked and felt dreamy.

The year before our expected departure, we dined with a gracious Italian couple who live and work in our town. Rich had become acquainted with them through the local Rotary Club. Vince and his wife Fausta offered many valuable tips at dinner that evening, but one of the most important concerned rental prices. When negotiated for longer than one month, the cost can be considerably less.

At first I imagined we'd have to fly to Italy to make the arrangements in person which, of course, would eat up any savings gained in a lower rent. It occurred to me to write to Rotary International. Surely they'd be happy to be a conduit between two Rotarians from different countries. Rotary headquarters responded quickly and kindly – they were sorry, but they were not a real estate agency.

Soon after we'd had dinner with Vince and Fausta, Rich and I enrolled in an Italian language class offered locally at a "Lifelong Learning" center. In the midst of one class, while some twenty adults took turns sputtering simple sentences describing their families in Italian, an idea popped into my head. Being seated in the back of the room gave me time to think while the others spoke. When my turn came, I hesitated. Lillian, the instructor, looked to me expectantly, chin raised, as teachers are wont to do. I no longer viewed her as a teacher, however. In my mind, she'd become a translator – a translator of the *letter* I had conjured while waiting my turn. I was so excited by my letter, I bumbled through a description of my family. I didn't care.

On the way home from class I could hardly wait to throw the idea out to Rich. "What if," I asked, "we wrote a letter, in Italian, with Lillian's help, describing the kind of housing we are looking for and e-mailed it to every Rotary Club in Italy?"

Within a day we'd composed the letter in rudimentary Italian, outlining the features we'd like in an apartment: one bedroom (preferably two), kitchen, living room and bathroom, within walking distance of town, and a panoramic view if at all possible. We also stated how much we could pay per month. Lillian kindly edited it as we had hoped she would. And off it went to 100 Rotary clubs in Italy.

Nearly fifty e-mails boomeranged back, marked "undeliverable." We received several replies from Italian Rotarians in the real estate business. They offered lovely places for the prohibitive $1,000-$5,000 per week.

We also received several responses from beautiful, warm and dry Sicily, but our Italian teacher said, "Forget it. Sicilians speak an entirely different dialect. They'll understand you (which I thought was a generous assumption on her part), but you won't understand them."

The one response that stood out from all the others came from a man named Giuseppe. In Italian, his e-mail explained that he lived in Bologna, but continued to own (and occasionally occupy) the house he'd grown up in two hours south in a city called Città di Castello. He had remodeled it into apartments, complete with modern conveniences and, at the same time, had maintained the old-style atmosphere and décor. He explained he didn't ordinarily allow anyone to stay in the apartment since it contained precious family memorabilia and, besides, he often used it himself. He would, however, make an exception for his "Rotarian friends." Città di Castello (Castle City) and the area, he said, were "most beautiful."

He and the apartment sounded too good to be true so, of course, we were skeptical. Never having heard of Città di Castello, we rushed to map it. It is smack-dab in the heart of Italy, ten miles east of Tuscany, in the province of Umbria. We would learn later that this fertile Upper Tiber River Valley had been dubbed "The Green Heart of Italy."

The more we corresponded with Giuseppe, the more excited Rich and I became. After the third communication, Giuseppe asked if we would like to see photos. Uh, yes!

The day we received the pictures in the mail, our anticipation heightened. Not only was the so-called "house" a mansion – an old mansion with a wrought-iron fence around it – but the rooms appeared spacious, comfortable and well-appointed. With the help of a phone call from Rotarian Vince from this side of the pond, to Giuseppe on the other, we came to an agreement with Giuseppe who would give us our much-needed start in Italy. Whew!

The Consulate required one more thing. We had to prove we were married, even though the marriage had occurred in the previous century. This requirement, the marriage certificate, led me to a shocking discovery. Sifting through our files of birth, death and ownership documents, I found the Catholic Church's certification of the legitimacy of our vows but not the legal document. I asked Rich if he thought the Catholic Church's stamp of approval would suffice since the country we were petitioning surrounds Vatican City. He shook his head.

Immediately, the visage of dear old Father Bennett, the priest who married us, popped into my head. Had he remembered to file the paperwork with Cook County, Illinois, thirty-two years ago? A couple phone calls later and "Bravo!" to both Father Bennett and the recordkeeping staff of Cook County. Our marriage certificate existed. When it arrived in the mail a few days later, Rich and I stared at it together. I don't know what he was thinking, but I questioned how my usually organized self had overlooked such an important task as getting our marriage certificate.

Back to Mr. and Mrs. Mayle. Never do we see them learning to speak French. To watch the movie one would think these Britons were born with champagne tongues. Rich and I, however, after taking the "Lifelong Learning" Italian, went on to spend two hours per week for 16 weeks at a community college, mumbling and bumbling through beginning and intermediate Italian. The hardest part was trying to forget the Spanish we'd learned in high school and college. Translating became a three-step English-Spanish-Italian process. For example, "mirror" → "el espejo" → "lo specchio." Contrary to what most people say, Spanish and Italian are not nearly identical. At least not to a beginner. The word "camino" means "pathway" in Spanish. In Italian, "camino" means "chimney." Can no one see the difference?

Another thing we won't understand in Italy is its politics. Both Rich and I love politics. We're addicted to national and international news. Whether there's an upcoming election or no election in sight, makes no difference. We're going to save so much time in Italy by not understanding what's going on we may actually have time for more leisurely pursuits, such as three-hour dinners, afternoon naps, and evening strolls. Whenever I picture our life in Italy, I imagine us walking a country road to town.

Meanwhile, our lives here in the States keep slipping away and, upon our departure, our two precious kitties, Skagway and Siena, will inherit our house. Our son Matt and his wife Hai Yan, who currently live in Beijing, China, will live in our house and take care of it so our cats will live the same lifestyle to which they are accustomed. You know, like the one we hope to find in Italy.

However, Matt and Hai Yan's planned arrival here in January has hit some snags. Hai Yan's visa hasn't arrived. As a Chinese citizen, she needs a visa to come to the U.S., even though she's married to an American. The delay worries me something awful because if she doesn't get her visa, they won't come and who will love and feed our kitties? Never mind that Matt is enrolled in classes that start at Wayne State University, in Detroit, on January 10, and he is supposed to drive us to the airport the following day. Never mind that every time I start getting excited about going to heaven I remember Hai Yan's darn visa.

Gentle and beautiful Hai Yan has passed the scrutiny of Homeland Security, complete with background criminal check, medical clearance and fingerprinting. She still needs the go-ahead to be interviewed by U.S. Immigration & Naturalization Services. The interview will take place in a city 1,200 miles away from Beijing where they live. In other words, even though there is a U.S. Embassy in Beijing, Matt and Hai Yan need to fly a distance equivalent to that between Detroit and Tampa for her interview. This red tape *cazzate* – pardon my Italian – is the spoiler amidst an otherwise exciting time.

Will such red tape exist in Italy? Of course it will, but we'll be like children, not understanding a bit of it, merrily living each moment. Besides, just like when we're on vacation, everything we normally view as an obstacle in the States will be considered an adventure there.

There's another interesting feeling rising in me. For some reason, I feel compelled to leave the house clean. The compulsion is as strong as the nesting instinct experienced right before the onset of labor. Don't ask me why I'm concerned the house will be clean because my son won't care one whit and everything will look so new and different to Hai Yan she probably won't even notice. Perhaps this drive to clean derives from either my half-German/half-Lithuanian ancestry or America's puritanical history. All I know is I've washed windows until they gleam, cleaned the cupboards, and uncluttered the basement (at least to the point one can when living with a packhorse).

Our son hasn't lived here since he was eighteen years old (he's 32 now), so I'm certain he doesn't know where the circuit breakers are, the water shutoff, or even where I store the light bulbs. The last time he resided here we lived in the olden days, cutting the grass with a push mower. This last realization is what inspired me to type up a "What's What" and a "Where's What" list for every room and gadget in the house, garage and yard. Since Matt left for college, even our garbage pickup day has changed.

Of course there are things I will miss, especially since I would be quite content to continue living the life I live now. My husband is the one with wanderlust; I'm the homebody. The mere planning for this transition has forced me to consciously release my grip on all my "stuff" and come to realize, with gratitude, what I'm leaving behind: the house and community that have been home to me for the majority of my life, the innocent kitties who have chosen to live with us and yet have no say in our leave-taking, and my job at the library. If truth be told, there's no place I'd rather be than in a library.

I'll also miss the Monday night discussions of "A Course in Miracles" at Renaissance Unity church and my twice monthly writers' group meetings. Sure, my fellow writers will still have the opportunity to critique my work via the Internet, but I'll so miss the banter and the laughter of our meetings. I'll miss strawberry picking in June and celebrating our December birthdays with my good friend Nadine, and sipping coffee with my other best bud, Katie, as we seek to further our understanding of English in our two-person Vocabulary Support Group (VSG). I'll miss the sweetest mother- and sister-in-law a woman could have and my darling daughter Chelsea, all of whom live in Chicago. I imagine what it would be like to never see any of them again and my appreciation for each deepens. If I dwell on this thought too long, my heart sinks to the floor, and I want to smash it with my heel for giving me so much pain.

The one thing I will not miss by being away from the United States is its atmosphere of fear. We have a radio station in Detroit that dubs itself "Your Winter Survival Station" months before winter arrives. Survival? In Detroit? Does a slow commute to work jeopardize one's survival? Does shoveling several inches of snow, or more likely, plowing several inches of snow, jeopardize one's survival?

In Italy I plan to shed the negative images of myself that belong to a past that no longer exists. In this new place I will dance and sing with abandon (heck, nobody will know me there), run when my body wants to run, sit silent when it wants to digest what art or food or conversation it has taken in. I will no longer cling to sameness which only gives me the illusion of safety. This is the opportunity of my lifetime, just like all the others that preceded it. I'm grateful for every single one of them and do not take my blessings lightly.

This is the time when I plan to learn to talk to the universe and, more importantly, take the time to listen to its reply; connect with nature as I did as a child; and recognize and acknowledge the life in everything, even the infinitesimal vibrations of rocks along the road. I plan to return to this country carrying myself as the blessed being I am. Italy, here I come. ♥

Update: Due to the delay in getting Hai Yan's visa, she and Matt didn't arrive in the U.S. until August! Between January and August, we hired Pat, our wonderful pet sitter, who also watched our house.

2

Arriving in "Castle City"

A little over a year after Rich's retirement, we fly to Rome. We don't set off for our new home in Umbria right away. Instead, Rich insists we tour the city for a couple days, which drives me crazy. We've toured Rome on two previous occasions, and I can hardly wait to see our new quarters. I so want to get "home" that it occurs to me that my nesting instinct may be over-developed.

These two days in Rome are like those leading up to Christmas – filled with dazzling sights, delectable tastes and smells and unbridled childlike anticipation. Still, I can't bring myself to live in the moment. My mind keeps racing ahead.

When the big day finally arrives, we take a cab from our hotel to the train station. This, alone, makes it special. Usually Rich convinces me the train station is close to the hotel and we schlep our luggage across busy four-lane streets, haul it over bumpy cobblestones through throngs of people and arrive at the station soaked in perspiration. Not only that, my head and face sweat like nobody's business. This time, though, since we'd packed for a year (two humungous and two large suitcases, Rich's carry-on and my laptop computer), even he conceded the necessity of a cab.

Standing amidst a crowd of people at Track 12, waiting for the train that will stop in Arezzo, where we plan to meet our sponsor Giuseppe, we hear an announcement. The train is not coming in on Track 12, where, as luck would have it, we stand at the farthest end of the platform. It will, instead, come in on Track 9. Ay yi yi!

I look across the way to Track 9 where the train is rolling to a stop. If it leaves on time, it will rumble out in precisely three minutes. Alarm must have registered on our faces for a woman approaches and offers help. Our choice is to either trust her not to run off with our luggage or miss the train. We opt for trust.

Arriving breathless at Track 9, Rich and I have no need to communicate – we've done this drill before. I, the "receiver," dash up the steps of the train and Rich, the "quarterback," hefts and passes the luggage onto the top step where I drag it farther inside to make space for the next piece. The woman who helps us will be the first of hundreds of angels we'll meet in the coming year.

The moment we settle into our seats we go to work on the next challenge – figuring out where to get off. When the conductor comes to punch our tickets, we first verify we've boarded the correct train and then ask how long it will be before we reach Arezzo. I try to settle back for the two-hour ride, allowing the Italian language from fellow passengers to burble over me. Still my nerves jangle. I stop and witness my nerves. They're not emanating from fear but from anticipation. We haven't even arrived, and already I sense a change.

Before we left, I renamed myself, ostensibly because many Italians seemed stymied on our previous visits by the letter "y" in Nancy. Although they're familiar with words such as "yoga" and "yogurt," the letter "y" is not in their alphabet. Their word for it is the Greek "epsilon." More importantly, spending a year in Italy feels like a fresh start. Like everyone, I've had some rough spots in my life and this is an opportunity to remove those spots – not the memory of them, but the stain of them.

I've often heard artists say how the light in Italy is different. Since the idea of "seeing things in a new light" appeals to me, I adopt the name Lucia (light) and, in honor of my given name, Nancy (a derivative of Ann), I added Anna. Combined, *Luciana* means "graceful light"; something to which I can aspire.

It's fun — recreating oneself. Of course, given the American tendency toward Puritanism, it must be a sin. That's one reason I so love Italy. They only talk about sin in church. The people of Italy appear to live totally free from useless hand-wringing guilt, indulging in all manner of pleasures such as languorous meals, uplifting music, leathering their skin in the sunshine, drinking wine like it is water, and enjoying sex. How outrageously celestial!

For me, recreating myself is about dumping fear and replacing it with surrender. And I don't mean "surrender" as in "giving up." I see surrender as letting go of preconceived outcomes and opening up more to spirit-inspired outcomes.

I learned about the choice between fear and surrender when we traveled to China for Matt and Hai Yan's wedding. Being as helpless as a toddler there, I had no choice but to follow my mother-in-law's example. Over the decades, whenever she traveled with us, she flowed with the experience. She never tried to change or resist it. Without exception, she trusted everything. In China, I finally started to get the hang of it. The result was joy — unbounded. It's the boundaries of familiarity and the fear of fear that keep me both yearning for and clinging to the imprisonment of my daily routine.

Really, I've been so shortsighted. I read recently that even the death of a body's cells is a blessing. Each day, whether we're aware of it or not, our body is new, rejuvenated, unlike the body we lived in the day before. Do we really want to live forever in a static state? Body cells that refuse to issue their own death warrant are known as cancer cells. Even as our bodies die, we create. Even as we die to one form of living, we renew to another. It's not even necessary to move to another country to experience such a transformation. We can create it in our daily lives by doing something life enhancing, something that makes us stretch, by reading something we're scared might challenge our way of thinking, by watching while consciously being open to seeing things differently, by questioning our beliefs.

A little over two hours after leaving Rome, we arrive in Arezzo. Before dragging all our stuff off the train, though, I confirm with not one, but three passengers that this stop is indeed Arezzo.

Out on the platform, penned like pigs by our luggage, we see that we must go downstairs and walk underground to bypass walking on the tracks. A man in uniform stands sentinel to keep people from taking a shortcut over the tracks. An elevator, which travels from the platform down to the underground walkway, is too small for our luggage, so we (well, okay, Rich) drags it off the platform and down the stairs to the tunnel and back upstairs to the lobby.

It is time to phone Giuseppe. Inside the train station I buy a phone card and, thanks to some travel writer's brilliant note, I know to break off the tip of the card before inserting it into the station's public phone. If the tip isn't broken off, it won't work. Why the clerk doesn't do that before he hands it to you I'll never know.

Giuseppe answers the phone on the first ring.

"Pronto!"

"Buon giorno! Sono Luciana."

"Ehhh! Luciana! Come stai?"

"Bene, e Lei?"

"Bene, bene. Dove sei?"

"Arezzo."

"Parto adesso. Ci vediamo subito, quarantacinque minuti. Ciao." (I'm leaving now. We'll see each other shortly, in 45 minutes. Bye.)

Rich and I try to relax in the coffee bar connected to the station, our luggage piled around us, sipping the best coffee I've ever tasted. We are so geeked the extra caffeine probably isn't such a good idea. Here we are, about to be driven to our new digs, and we don't know much about Giuseppe: what he looks like, if he speaks English, what his driving record is.

Blindsiding me and nearly scaring me to death, Giuseppe rushes up, holds out his arms to me and, smiling, yells, *"Ehhh!"* as Italians frequently do. I rise and wrap my arms around this short, pushing seventy, human dynamo. He gives me the two-cheeked Italian kiss and then holds out his hand to shake Rich's. He has a full head of auburn hair, à la Ronald Reagan, wears glasses and flashes a dazzling smile. He is a sunbeam!

Before we have a chance to say anything, Giuseppe grabs a couple pieces of our heavy luggage and is hauling them out of the café. We gather up the rest and follow. His car is a small silver hatchback – a *very* small hatchback. Instantly I notice Giuseppe's determination to stuff every last piece of luggage and all three of us into it, even if it means me being squished in a corner of the backseat, my shoulders folding in on themselves, and Rich sitting in the passenger seat, his eyes barely peeking over the suitcase on his lap. It is tucked so snugly between the dashboard and his lap that he risks losing circulation in his legs. One thing for sure, we are packed in so tight that if the car crashes, we'll still be in our seats when the dust settles.

The three of us make conversation as best we can during the ride on a two-lane highway through hills and valleys. Giuseppe knows little English and we know little Italian. As a result, it is fairly quiet in the car, which is good since it gives us time to enjoy the beautiful hills, mountains and valleys of first Tuscany, and then, as we ride farther east, Umbria. The area surrounding Città di Castello is breathtaking with its Apennine Mountains, and it is only January. Giuseppe was right. This area of Italy is *molto bellissima*.

⁘

When we pull into the gravel driveway of a stately house, I can't believe our good luck. The three-story stucco is magnificent. Just as important, the medieval wall surrounding the historic district of Città di Castello stands directly across the street from the mansion.

A bakery and gas station are to the right of the imposing structure, and a bank sits on the other side. Giuseppe pulls up the gravel drive, hops out of the car and swings open the heavy iron gate, slides back into the car and drives up to the door. He leads us through the tall wooden front doors, up the worn marble stairs, through another set of locked doors. He shows us around what used to be his apartment but will now be ours for the first

The stucco mansion.

couple months, until we find our own place. One room, the dining room where family heirlooms and historical documents are stored, will be locked to us. Still, the remaining space encompasses more than we dared hope for. The photos he'd sent hadn't done this place justice.

Giuseppe gives us a crash course on how everything works – from the thermostat to the silver stove-top coffeemaker. Thoughtfully, he's taped a map of the town to the kitchen wall and circled the places he thinks we'll need most, among them his favorite restaurants. He plans to spend the night in the apartment below this one. He leaves us to unpack and get settled. Soon after, he returns to deliver a cooked duck and a loaf of Italian bread – something we really appreciate since it is late afternoon and we are starving. Three hours later, after sun set, he returns to lead us on a tour of the neighborhood. Knowing we won't have a car during our stay, he walks us to the supermarket three blocks away where we pick up a few staples. Deciphering the labels seems to take forever. We are grateful for the pictures

Giuseppe.

on the products.

Once in a while I glance at Giuseppe who stands off to the side, hands folded in front of him. Each time he smiles, shakes his head a little and looks down at the floor as if he can't believe we actually came.

I can't believe it either.

After putting the groceries away, Giuseppe takes us across the street where we enter the walls of the Renaissance city. We could not be more thrilled. It has everything, complete with piazzas, clothing stores, restaurants, an Internet/telephone store, fresh fruit-and-vegetable market, city hall, seven churches, a cathedral, hundreds of bells and a deep sense of history. He treats us to dinner at one of his favorite restaurants where I taste my first freshly made pasta. It melts in my mouth. The wine warms me through to my bones.

After dinner we walk out of the historic district, and cross the street to our new home. Giuseppe must sense my excitement for he allows me to swing open the heavy wrought-iron gate. I run up the two steps and, for the first time, unlock the gigantic door. As I push it open, I feel as though I've fallen into a Fellini movie set. Living in an apartment proves you don't have to rent a villa to feel the romance of Italy. ❤️

3

HEAVENLY DINNER

The first Sunday after we arrive, friends of Giuseppe's ask him to invite us to their home inside the walls of Città di Castello. The time is set for 6:30 p.m. Even though Italians don't eat dinner until eight, we suspect we're being invited for a meal. I figure the gathering will begin with drinks and antipasti and by 7:30 or 8 we'll be dining.

I ask Giuseppe if we should change into nicer clothes for the evening, and he shakes his head. I'm relieved since my dressier clothes are still in transit in the boxes we mailed from the United States. I envision them on a ship in the middle of the Atlantic.

Before going to Giuseppe's friends' house, we spend a whirlwind day with him. Despite his age, he is one of those people compelled to keep moving, and to keep moving quickly. Much to his credit, though, he patiently deciphers our extremely limited Italian. He drives us to several nearby hill towns to give us a feel for the area. If some place strikes our fancy, we can always return on our own by bus or train. After all, an entire year stretches out before us.

After Giuseppe's tour, the three of us walk single-file through a maze of narrow cobblestone streets in Città di Castello's historic district. Knots of people gather to socialize. To allow space for vehicles to pass, our shoulders brush the walls of the stone buildings as we walk. It's mid-January, and darkness fell over an hour ago.

The wood smoke slithering from Renaissance chimneys stings my nose. The crystal-clear sky sports a crescent moon. The temperature, especially biting due to high winds and the tunnel effect created by the tall narrow corridors of the buildings, keeps us moving quickly and without conversation. It amazes me how crowded it is.

Finally, Giuseppe stops at a large door and rings the bell. Buzzed in, we step into a grand foyer that feels dank compared to the crisp air outside. Up the wide circular staircase and round the bend stands Liana Curzio, dressed in a fine wool two-piece sweater-and-skirt set. Her necklace and earrings sparkle in the light cast from the hallway's grand chandelier.

Liana's brown eyes and warm smile welcome us inside where my nose expects to smell the beginnings of supper. Instead, I inhale warmed air, thick with chimney smoke. A cat strolls over to see who's visiting.

We shake hands with Liana and her husband Quinto, a wiry man with olive skin, Roman nose, bald head and a gray mustache and beard. Liana says something about Quinto. I pick out the words "sick" and "fever." I think maybe we should let them off the hook and suggest we return another time. They insist we stay.

They escort us from the entry hall through the small kitchen where a brick stove burns wood. Two chairs sit close to the fire, which seems to indicate the couple spends most of their time here. We continue through a floor-to-ceiling door, tall enough for a giraffe to walk through, into a small parlor. The air is cooler here. We follow through yet another giraffe door into a living area the size and height of a ballroom. It is decidedly much cooler here.

We are told the ceiling beams are original, dating to the 1200s. We crane our necks and study them open-mouthed. Their rough-hewn appearance coupled with their thickness leave Rich and me in awe. An entire wall of heavy wooden bookcases flank the room on the left. Two paintings of nudes, a fireplace and family photos flank the right. Four armless contemporary white sofas form two "Ls" around a large, low, glass coffee table.

After we take our seats, Liana asks if we are comfortable. I nod as a

Quinto and Liana.

draft wraps itself around my ankles. While Rich has a wide temperature tolerance range, mine is rigidly narrow. I wonder if Quinto wishes he were back in front of the wood-burning chimney and worry he might be more susceptible to catching a chill. As if he reads my mind, he hurries off and quickly returns with a gray wool cap pulled over his head. He gestures to the photos hanging on the whitewashed walls. Rich and I rise to take a closer look. I'm startled to see that Quinto's collection includes photos of both his grandparents and great grandparents.

Records of my family history pale next to his. I have a few photos of the grandfather I knew as a child and one of his wife … taken of her lying in an open casket outside a Catholic church on the south side of Chicago. I wonder what factor in Quinto's and my histories left him with old photos and me with virtually none.

What makes me especially envious is that Quinto and Giuseppe went through school together, having attended the grade school within these walls where Giuseppe's mother had taught. Ah, I think – to have my best grade-school friend so close to me for over six decades. Suddenly, I feel

19

overly mobile, and up until now, Rich and I have only lived in two places over a 32-year-period. Liana has lived in this huge four-story manse her entire life, as did her parents.

After admiring the family photos, Liana leads us to a table at the far side of the spacious room next to the window. Everyone takes a seat except her. She serves tea in midnight blue gold-rimmed china. A gold flower motif decorates each cup. I'm surprised. Here we are in coffee country and we're being served tea. Not that I mind given the temperature in the room. Anything hot is welcome.

Liana stands at the window and gestures to me. When I start to get up, she repeats the gesture. I'm confused. I interpret her hand motion, with palm down and fingers waving back and forth, to mean I should stay seated, yet the rest of her clearly says "come here." Finally, I overcome my conditioning and listen to my instincts. Reluctantly, I unclench my fingers from around the still-warm cup and join her at the window. I can't help noticing how the fingertips of her left hand lightly rest on the ice-cold radiator. How cold does it have to be before they put the heat on? With her other hand, she points to something outside. When I lean closer to the window to look, I see the three towers that grace Città di Castello. She tells me this is a rare sighting. Months later, I come to understand what she meant. There are few vantage points where all three towers can be seen at once.

Back in my seat, I find it difficult to follow the conversation. Everyone talks so fast – or at least that's what it sounds like – fast talk. Once I ask them to speak more slowly, though, I am able to understand Liana a little. It is obvious Quinto is so excited to see his good

The three towers of Città di Castello.

friend Giuseppe that he chatters on with him and takes only a passing, polite interest in us. That's okay with me since I'm having a hard enough time keeping up with Liana.

Liana rises and disappears. When she returns, something heavenly happens. She adds to this table, warming me in an unforgettable way, a bowl of amaretto cookies (tiny enough to pop into your mouth like popcorn), bowls heaping with foil-wrapped chocolates and a buttery yellow cake, thickly daubed with chocolate frosting. Liana, good hostess that she is, serves everyone two pieces of cake to start! As if by holy intervention, I start to understand more of what is being said, and I am living my childhood dream of eating sweets for dinner. To top it off, I'm sitting in a huge, four-story structure situated on land where the Romans once ruled, and before them, the Etruscans. Add to this the fact that by evening's end Liana introduces me to all three of her cats and Quinto's dog, "Deke," and I am thoroughly content.

When it is time to leave, Liana puts on her coat and follows us downstairs with "Deke" on his lead. Before going outside, she shows us Quinto's first-floor law office (the size of a large basement) with whitewashed walls, nicely appointed art and furniture and a large glass desk. Then she and "Deke" walk the three of us home.

With Giuseppe in an apartment on the first floor, and us on the second floor, Rich says he's still hungry. He prepares eggs and toast for himself while I lollygag on the couch. I determine not to ruin the buttery chocolaty taste lingering so delectably in my mouth. Not knowing at the time why we were only served sweets for "dinner," I ponder this miraculous event and decide not to question it but to sit back and enjoy it. I eat nothing else before going to bed, and even leave my teeth unbrushed. ♥

Update: Weeks later we learn that Italians consume such a large meal on Sunday afternoons that they eat little or nothing for dinner. This explained the early evening repast of tea and sweets.

4

GROCERY SHOPPING IN WINTER

Apart from the supermarket Giuseppe had shown us upon our arrival, we find another one inside the city walls. The European franchise, called the UPIM (pronounced *ooh-peem*), sits tucked in an ancient concrete edifice on a pedestrian-only street. Baby buggies and unlocked bicycles clutter each side of the entranceway.

We follow an old woman wearing a fur coat over her black dress. Bent with years, she easily climbs the steps to get inside. These steps, and all the millions of others sprinkled, seemingly pell-mell, throughout small-town Italy, do not deter the handicapped or aged from getting out and about. The intrepid Italians make Americans circling a parking lot in search of a space right next to the store look silly.

The grocery store.

On this January morning, stepping into the UPIM is like stepping into a freezer. The temperature inside the store is colder than outdoors. We'll soon learn that in addition to grocery stores, Italians do not heat their cafés, department stores, clothing stores, internet/telephone stores, most restaurants (even fancy-schmancy ones), flower shops, bakeries, or hardware stores.

To keep warm, I quickly acquire a taste for wine, which delights Rich.

In previous visits I always ordered Coca-Cola, which costs more than wine. Rich is in no way stingy, but he could never get past my ordering a cola when wine runs like water here.

You might think stores are not heated because Italy is always sunny and warm, but that belief springs from the illusion Hollywood has so successfully planted in our American heads. The winter months are cold, damp and chilly. It even snows, often, although it doesn't pile up in northern Umbria the way it piles up in southeast Michigan.

Italians appear oblivious to the cold. Store clerks resemble penguins hunkered down in merino wool turtlenecks, puffy quilted coats, and gloves with the fingertips cut off. The butchers and deli staff wear neither coats nor sweaters. Aprons cover their long-sleeved T-shirts. Though I don't understand Italian, I am sure no one is complaining about the temperature and none of the shoppers seems frazzled or hurried.

At first glance, the UPIM appears to be similar to small groceries in the United States, but upon closer inspection, differences abound. For one thing, it closes every afternoon between 1 and 4 p.m. Rich and I have lost count of the number of times he's set off to buy food only to return empty handed. Not only does he forget the store closes every afternoon when, not so ironically, we have time on our hands, but he also forgets that this particular store is closed all day Sundays *and* Thursdays. Even worse, I allow him to go without so much as a question, completely forgetting the hours myself. One would think that between the two of us, at least one would remember.

The initial aisle of the four-aisled store features fruit and vegetables. The moment I pick up an apple to inspect it, another shopper hands me a paper-thin plastic glove. Looking around, I see others similarly donning gloves before touching the produce. This surprises me since Italians don't seem phobic about germs and they peel nearly all their fruit and vegetables before eating them anyway.

After choosing two apples and bagging them, I dare not do another thing until taking time to observe. I watch as they place their bags of produce on a scale, press a white button and then a green button. The machine spits out a sticky label with the name and price of the item, which they affix to the bag. When finished in the produce aisle, they strip off the glove and throw it in the nearby trash can.

Simple enough. I step up to the scale, place my bag of apples on it, then panic. Rows of numbers, 1 through 100, stare back at me. I don't know which one to press. I turn to the person waiting behind me and look askance. The woman steps forward, peers inside my sack, turns on her high heels and click-clicks to the crate from which I'd plucked the apples. Facing me, she kindly points to the number next to the price sign, which indicates the type of produce I'd chosen.

I say, "*Grazie.*"

She smiles and replies, "*Prego.*"

I catch up to Rich, patiently reading labels on bottles in the olive-oil aisle, all of which brims with choice. Being a "foodie," he likes to read labels in America as well.

Across the aisle I see glass bottles of Coca-Cola. I pick one up. My goodness, it's the same small size as the five-cent sodas we used to drink when we were kids. Oh, I think, it will be so easy to keep the weight off here. I am concerned, though, about getting enough fiber. I'm not fond of root vegetables and it's winter and Italians eat according to the season.

I nudge Rich. He looks up from the bottle of *aceto* (vinegar) he's holding and follows my pointing finger toward cartons of eggs. They're stacked right out in the open; not in the refrigerated section. My thinking goes from, *Yes, that's smart since it's so cold in here* to *Don't they freeze at night?* Rich shakes his head in wonderment and goes back to reading the label.

Although the produce, cheese, wine and olive oil sections of the store brim with choices, the bread aisle merely appears to offer choice. Shelf upon shelf of white bread come in every size and shape imaginable. Not one, though, helps fulfill the USDA Food Pyramid's largest rectangle regarding fiber. Over time we buy one loaf after another. Each and every one lacks salt. And taste. The Umbrians haven't recalibrated since the Middle Ages when salt was scarce. This turns out to be a good thing for bread-and-butter inhaling people like me. The amount of bread I consume falls dramatically and aids in reducing my paunch which is important since I'm now drinking 100% more wine than before.

While still in the U.S., it had occurred to me that it would be fun to bake cookies in Italy. Since I wouldn't be working, I imagined baking a batch now and again for people who helped us along the way. Those who love to bake as I do, should be forewarned. First, there is absolutely no reason to bake a cake, pastry or cookies while in Italy. There are as many awe-inspiring bakeries in Italy as there are churches. Besides, grocery stores do not sell baking powder, cake mixes, cookie dough, chocolate chips, pastry flour, baking raisins, confectioners' sugar or canned frosting.

Moving on, our search for fiber-rich foods continues. No rice, except Arborio (for making risotto). Certainly no brown rice. Not counting the few sugary children's cereals on the shelves, we find nothing but corn flakes – the real McCoy, Kellogg, plus various versions of the same flake.

When I look over to Rich, he's disappeared. My eyes are drawn downward. Rich is on the floor on his hands and knees. I see him stretching to reach the way-back of the bottom shelf. As he straightens, still kneeling, a grin spreads across his face. He holds up his find: oatmeal. Real, honest-to-goodness stone-ground oatmeal. We high-five.

Once I realize that both Tuscany and Umbria can be cold, damp and chilly, I find myself, for the first time, feeling sorry for the Italians. What could they possibly eat for breakfast to make them feel as good all over as hot cereal or fiber-rich buttered toast? My pity for them dissipates the instant I learn their regular breakfast consists of a flaky, fruit- or cream-filled pastry washed down by a sweetened espresso, cafe-latte or cappuccino. It doesn't take me long to hop on that chuck wagon.

The store offers oodles of pasta. I'd heard there are more than two hundred kinds, all with different names, and I'll bet our vacation bank account that this store carries every single one. The thought of a vocabulary test on them gives me the shivers.

There's lots of space allotted for finely blended espresso coffee. Stuffed in between, an obvious afterthought, a box of loose tea.

The lowest grade milk is 1.5% fat (I drink 0% at home), and is labeled *scremato* ("low fat"). Each time I guzzle it I will lock my eyes on the word *scremato* to keep from feeling guilty. It's so delicious I wonder why it isn't packaged in cartons larger than quart size. Months later, after I've drunk barrels of it, we'll learn that though Italians drink milk, they consume it in much smaller quantities than Americans.

Lots of choices come in the cheese department. Piles of it. Boatloads of yogurt and butter, and chocolate candy from the capital of Umbria, Perugia, a specialty there. I recognize the foil-wrapped treats from the evening we spent with Liana and Quinto.

The deli case is chockfull of cured meats. Fresh buffalo mozzarella balls swim in dishes of liquid, as do olives (zillions of olives, in a hundred varieties), pickled vegetables and anchovies.

At checkout, I see the old woman we'd followed into the store. She is on her way out, a plastic tote in each hand, the weight of which seems to lengthen her arms.

We place our items on the conveyor belt. The seated grocery store clerk swipes our items across the scanner and shoves them down the ramp where we're accustomed to seeing a bagger standing at the ready. There are no baggers here, and the ramp where the groceries land is divided in two by a plastic bar. It puzzles me.

When the clerk speaks to us, we look at her blankly. She lifts up a plastic bag and raises an eyebrow. We nod. She asks how many, and we quickly assess the volume of our purchases and say two. She tosses the bags on top of our groceries. Rich pays and before I can even get one of the plastic bags open she's waiting on the next person, shoving their items on the other side of the bar dividing the ramp.

Looking at the receipt later, we see that we paid five *centesimi* for each bag. Since we can't find any tall kitchen garbage bags to buy, we're happy to have these. In the States, I always carry to the store a large vinyl bag with strong handles and receive a five-cent refund. While packing to move to Italy, I included that green bag thinking I'd be oh-so-European carrying it to the store each day. Now I'm here and see that only old ladies tote their own bags to the store.

As time passes, my grocery store list for products sold only in America keeps growing. I long to ask friends who are coming to visit to bring us whole wheat bread, skim (0% fat) milk, and whole wheat flour. Upon our more reasonable requests, guests will bring us other, more packable, items from my wish list, including, brown rice, maple syrup, Kashi cereal (12 g. fiber per one-cup serving) and envelopes of Good Seasons salad dressing. Italians toss every salad with olive oil and vinegar, no exceptions.

On our way out, while the customer behind us bags her groceries, she drops a glass jar on the floor. Crash! I turn around and stare at her feet. My eyes widen. Shock ripples up my spine. An explosion of red sauce covers her high heels and the floor. Not just any sauce but *Prego* Spaghetti sauce! I look at Rich and say, "I can't believe they sell *that* here," and we smile. ♥

Update: The following year many stores stop imitating American stores and cease providing plastic bags. Once again, customers, young and old, bring their own reusable bags. And at least one American supermarket adopts the ramp with a divider bar at checkout.

5

LOST IN CYBER-HELL

Before we left for Italy, we researched cell phones. Several travel-savvy Americans had recommended we purchase a couple from a well-known American phone company, but the monthly charges were high and it cost eighty-five cents a minute to call the U.S. from Italy. This did *not* fit into our budget, particularly because of a promise I'd made. To sell the idea of "Italy for a Year" to our relatives, I'd promised my mother-in-law, sister-in-law and daughter – all of whom live in Chicago – that our being in Italy would in no way disrupt our weekly calling schedule. I even promised to chat the same amount of time. We're talking well over an hour weekly here.

Another option for international calling involves using Italy's public telephones which requires buying a calling card from a *Tabaccaio*, like we did when we first arrived at the Arezzo train station and needed to call Giuseppe to pick us up. These state-run shops are ubiquitous throughout Europe – distinguished by their blue signs with a large white "T" on them. They sell a variety of things, such as candy, gum, envelopes, bus tickets, cigarettes, stamps and phone cards. This option is far less expensive. Public telephones, though, always seem to be situated in noisy places, such as bars or on busy street corners, where it is difficult to hear.

A few days after our arrival, we visit a telephone store in the main piazza of Città di Castello. Its slogan, "Living without Borders," sounds promising. We arrive in late afternoon, when the store reopens after its three-hour "siesta." (Yes, "siesta" is Spanish but that's also what the Italians call it.) By the time we purchase an inexpensive cell phone from a young man named Francesco, night has fallen. Francesco speaks some English, but still the process is long and tedious.

Before buying a second phone, we decide to use the first one awhile. It is the kind of phone where time is purchased up front and money can be added as needed. Additional time can be bought in two ways. Using a credit card, you can either call the company (not feasible since the instructions of "push this for that" and "push that for this" are in Italian) or pop into a store and have the clerk add it.

We bring this first phone to the apartment and, by trial and error, set up its auto-dial directory and settings. We're pleased with it. There is no land phone at the apartment, and we give up the idea of ordering one after learning it "only takes six months" to get one installed. Besides, we like the idea of having two cell phones so Rich and I can contact each other when we aren't together, which happens often. We never had a cell phone in Michigan, and now we are going to own two. Wait till our friends and children hear we've joined the 21st Century.

While Rich runs errands around town, I return to the cell phone store to buy a second, identical, phone from Francesco. Afterward, at home in the apartment, I call Rich's mother in Chicago to see if it works okay. In the middle of our conversation, the phone dies. I try calling back but keep getting a message, first in Italian followed by English, saying, "This client is not approved for this kind of call." Since we'd put fifty euros' worth ($75) of time on it, and I'd already reached Mom once, I keep trying again and again as if it will magically correct itself.

The following Monday I return to Francesco and before I can open my mouth, he nods and says, "*Non funziona, sì?*" ("Doesn't work, yes?")

"*Sì. Sì,*" I nod.

He says the system hasn't accepted the registration of the second phone. It will take a few days to straighten out what he refers to as a "cyber-space" problem. Whenever he describes it, which he does repeatedly, he looks at the ceiling and whirls his forefinger above his head. Despite the language barrier, we both agree no problem is harder to solve than one floating willy-nilly in cyberspace.

I return every day for a week. Each time I enter the store Francesco shakes his head, holds up my paperwork, which always seems to be at his fingertips. "I call every day," he says. I believe him.

After more than a week, I've had it. Having been an American teenager during the 1960s sit-in demonstrations, I plan to return the phone, ask for a new one, and if none appears, I will stay there and *aspetto* – wait. If lunch time and its subsequent closing for siesta arrives, someone will have to drag me out of there. I pray to end the helpless feeling of being a victim of cyber-space hell and, at the same time, not become a victimizer. After all, I will be dealing with a live human being – a sweet, easy-on-the-eyes young man

who sincerely wants to help us purchase two functioning cell phones. Before leaving the apartment, I shower, put on makeup, fresh clothes and pack a novel. Sit-ins can take time.

I am not concerned Francesco will consider me strange – he already knows that. The night we bought the first phone we'd been in the store so long I'd forgotten what day of the week it was. When Rich and I turned to leave, I'd also forgotten about the step down to the door that exits into the main piazza. I missed the step altogether, tumbled forward, banged my left hand black-and-blue against a clear

Francesco in front of the telephone store. Note the step inside the store and how the door opens inward. Propping it open is a container for wet umbrellas.

plastic display case, continued to hurtle forward with a head slam into the glass floor-to-ceiling window only to come to a stop after my right hand bammed into the front door. The glass window vibrated so long I feared it might loosen from its casing and fall to the ground, or worse, on my head, like a sheet of water tumbling over a waterfall. For a moment I saw stars. Regaining my balance, I looked back and saw horror etched on Rich's face. Francesco and his female cohort had risen a few inches from their seats, watching round-eyed over the counter.

Fortunately, my head is hard, no damage done, and I thanked God I hadn't twisted my ankle, an oft-repeated trick of mine while on holiday.

My pratfall could have been much more dramatic had I been in a U.S. store. In Italy, nearly every exterior door opens inward instead of outward. Had the door been an American one, whereby the people inside the store could quickly escape in case of, say, a fire, my body probably would have been propelled out into the main piazza. The fact that the door had to be pulled inward for a person to exit, stole some drama from the incident.

So here I am, entering the store for the umpteenth time, the sentence "I want a new phone, I want a new phone" firmly planted in my head in Italian ("*Vorrei un nuovo telefono.*"). It has been my mantra for twenty-four hours. I'm determined not to leave the store until I receive a functioning phone.

Upon entering, I thank God – no other customers, no other salesperson. Only Francesco. I need his undivided attention. We chat the polite preliminaries, and move on to the problem, shaking our heads in commiseration.

I ask a series of questions. "Have you called customer service?" Yes, but no luck. "Have you talked to your manager?" She doesn't know what to do about it. "Has this ever happened before?" Yes, once in awhile, but usually these problems resolve themselves within three days.

He says that whenever he has a free moment, he calls computer headquarters, sometimes hourly, to see if the mystery has been solved. He explains that every time they put my information in, "The computer goes ..." and then he waggles his hands in front of his stomach, as if it is in turmoil. I interpret this to mean it is I who makes the system act squirrelly.

Time to employ my mantra. "I want a new phone." He explains that a new phone will not solve the problem. I ask, "Does it have anything to do with me buying two phones within a few days of each other?" His eyes brighten. Now we are getting somewhere. "What if my husband buys it instead of me?"

He hangs his head, wags it back and forth. *"Mi dispiace"* (I'm sorry), he says over and over again.

Just when I've strung out my questioning as long as I can, my knight in shining armor walks in. Rich raises his eyebrows and puts on that sweet grin of his as he looks askance from me to Francesco. I relay what has been said thus far. Francesco motions to me to come behind the counter. He points to his computer which indicates the untold number of calls he has logged on my behalf.

Rich asks Francesco, "What if you call customer service right now and ask for someone who speaks English?"

Francesco nods and picks up the phone. After what seems like five minutes of him explaining the problem to someone in ultra-rapid Italian, my eyes meet Rich's. We shrug. We have no idea what he is saying. Not once do I hear him ask for someone who speaks English. Put on hold, Francesco looks at us apologetically.

Running out of time before the stores close for the three-hour-lunch break, Rich sets off to run more errands. He always has a lot to do since he cooks dinner and needs to buy different foods from different places. He has already established "his" cheese lady, "his" fishmonger and "his" fresh pasta shop. I sit on one of the stools in front of Francesco's desk and stare out at the square with all its interesting people and dogs, praying, praying, no customer walks in to interrupt my mission.

Dogs, many belonging to store owners, run free inside the city walls. After observing the mutts awhile, I conclude they don't care one iota about the people or cars passing through. Their only interest is each other. New dog enters square, all dogs present run to greet it and smell it. They hang out in groups wherever they want, forcing pedestrian, bicycle, car and truck traffic to skirt around them. It occurs to me that their behavior mimics the people's, except for the smelling part.

Meanwhile, I hear Francesco continually feeding the person on the other end of the line my address in the U.S., my address in Italy, my passport number and my birth date. He repeats my birth date so often I figure he might remember to send me a birthday card.

When Rich returns, Francesco is still gripping the phone. Rich leaves again. Suddenly I detect hope in Francesco's voice. On and on the talking continues. I hold my breath. Rich returns again. Francesco hangs up.

"Is it solved?" I ask.

"Well, yes and no," Francesco says. In combination English/Italian he explains: "We can't get the system to accept your information but I can put it under your husband's name."

I can't believe it! Wasn't that what I'd asked earlier? Francesco says he can complete the process if Rich has his *documenti*, which means his passport. I look to Rich, who is reaching inside his leather jacket. He shakes his head. "It's in my other coat."

He leaves the store and jogs to the apartment. I head to the chair at the back of the store where I had planned to park myself during my sit-in. I take out my book and read. Fifteen minutes later, Rich returns. They don't need me for the transaction so I turn back to my book, happy I came prepared. ♡

Update: Seven months later we realize the telephone company, whose slogan is "Living Without Borders," sold us phones that could never make an outgoing international call (the one call to my mother-in-law in the beginning must've been a fluke). Similarly odd is the fact that we can receive incoming international calls at absolutely no charge. In addition, whenever we travel in a European country outside Italy, these phones are useless. We can't even use them to call each other. Technology – can't live with it, can't live without it.

Every Sunday afternoon, however, we call our relatives in the U.S. from a store named "Internet Point." It offers ten indoor telephone booths and only charges twelve cents a minute to call America and ten cents a minute to call China. But that's another story.

6

THAWING OUT IN THE LIBRARY

If I were forced to choose one place in the world in which to live out my days, it would be a library. I've given this a lot of thought, ruling out a beach or pool in Hawaii, a cabin in a Colorado pine forest and yes, even a villa in Italy. I figure that more than six months in any of those places would addle my brain and quash my desire to live. The content of a library, however, gives birth to new life and deeper levels of meaning with every reading.

The entrance to the library.

Regardless of where I am, this addiction leads me to the local library, and Città di Castello is no exception. My feet simply walk there. Hidden at the end of a narrow cobblestone road, I walk up five cement steps into a 17th Century building that formerly served as a convent. Inside, the low, barrel-vaulted ceiling oozes warmth. Its variegated pink-hued bricks rise up from opposing walls, arching until they meet in the middle.

A fiftyish woman sits behind the check-out counter. When she twirls her chair toward me, I ask, *"Dove si trova ..."* Before I can finish my question, she jumps out of her chair. With an open potato chip bag in her hand, she exits left from behind the counter, and walks in front of the counter past me to where it ends on the right. She climbs two steps and summons a librarian from her office. While watching this, I can't help but question the inefficiency of the arrangement. The opening should be on the right side of the counter. Even better would be a buzzer under the counter to ring staff. Then I remember we're in Italy.

A petite woman, wearing a ruffled blouse, jeans and three-inch high heels, emerges. Gingerly she navigates the steps down to my level. Her jet-black hair is loosely pinned in a swirl atop her head. Several stray strands drift past her ears to her shoulders. Her large eyes peek out from under a fringe of poker-straight bangs. Her angelic face and sweet voice belie her name, Diva.

When the first woman with the potato chips hears my entire question, *"Dove si trova la toiletta?"* she leads me into a hallway and points to the bathroom.

By the time I return to the front counter, Diva has disappeared. The first woman, now totally enthralled with stuffing as many potato chips into her mouth as possible, leans back deeply into her chair. I imagine her toes barely touching the floor. In Italian, I ask if there are any books in English. Her jaw stops, her hand stops moving inside the bag, and she stares at me. Then she hops up, wipes her hand on her pants, and again comes out from behind the counter, and walks its length to retrieve Diva. I wonder what in heaven's name this woman does at the library besides eat potato chips and summon Diva.

Eventually I come to realize she is a "library collectible." This type of patron is either eccentric and/or quirky, but has endeared her- or himself to staff who, in turn, take the person under their collective wing. It's important to clarify that although they tend to visit the library daily, not all patrons who visit daily are collectibles, or even candidates for collectibility.

In response to my inquiry about books in English, Diva motions to me to follow her. Thanks to the heavenly chocolate dinner at Liana and Quinto's house, I now understand the gesture for "come here" in Italy. She holds out her hand, palm down, and flaps her fingers down and up, down and up. I follow her through glass-paned French doors into the adult reading room.

A few people, seated at tables circa 1950, look up to see who has entered.

In a couple of minutes, Diva has plucked a half-dozen American and British classics from various shelves. She shows me the English on the left-hand page and the corresponding Italian on the right-hand page. Perfect. I ask if I may check out Oscar Wilde's *The Picture of Dorian Gray*.

She nods and we return to the check-out counter to issue me a library card. I am as giddy as the first time I applied for one.

What so fascinates me about reading is how much I immerse myself in each moment. I seem to be more present in the book's "sun-dappled forest" than when I'm actually standing in a sun-dappled forest. If only I could be as focused in my daily life as I am when my nose is in a book, I suspect I would not need as much time for reading and would spend more time living.

Since my presence at the cell phone store seemed to cause its computer to go on the fritz, I'm not surprised when the library's does the same thing. Diva calls for the help of a second librarian, Antonella. Both women murmur apologies and, when the computer does not respond after several minutes of gentle prodding, Antonella makes up a card by hand. Although she asks to see my passport, she does not ask for proof of where I live in Italy, a mandatory requirement where I work. While waiting, I luxuriate in the trust they give me.

All this happens before I tell them I work in a library. When I mention it conversationally, both Diva and Antonella's eyes widen. Their smiles broaden as if I've just told them we're blood relatives. Ever since then, I'm ashamed to admit, I've been given special treatment. Several months later, they even waive a ten-*centesimi* fine on an overdue book. Ssshh!

Since I'm genetically predisposed to be a homebody, having access to the Internet becomes a major requirement for my comfort while being away from home so long. I have a deep need to keep in touch with friends and family. I also need to pay our bills … on time. No one I know of in Città di Castello has Internet access in their own homes, so demand in public places is high.

Only three venues exist in Città di Castello where we can check our e-mail and surf the Internet: one public terminal at the library (time limit: one-half hour, no charge), one public terminal at a municipal office (time limit: one-half hour, no charge), and eight terminals at the Internet/telephone store, which we dub "The Cold Place" because, no matter the time of year, the owner props the doors wide open (no time limit, one-and-one-half euros per hour).

Of the three places with access, I like the library's best for several reasons, the first of which is that it's winter and the library is the only place I've found that turns on its heat. Although I've acquired a taste for wine, I don't want to get into the habit of drinking it at breakfast.

Second, navigating the Internet at the library is less annoying than at "The Cold Place" because its computer filters out pornographic pop-ups. Of course, any pop-up annoys me, but pornographic ones top my list. You might've thought this would have been my *first* reason for preferring the library's computer over others, but it's really hard to type with frozen fingers.

Third, the library provides plenty of desk space on which to spread out my things: checkbook, paper, pen, purse, gloves, etc. The problem with the library's computer is that it is rarely available; either it's down, or already occupied with a long waiting list.

Not having easy access to the Internet, plus 99.9% of everything inside the library being in Italian, means I have to find other excuses for hanging out there because not only do I love the place, but I also need somewhere to thaw out. I'm careful, though, not to act overly needy so as to avoid the risk of becoming a library collectible.

Recalling how I learned to read English, I walk up some steps to the children's room. I browse through a few third-grade books, but I can't even guess what the words mean. I pull a second-level book from the shelf and thumb through it. Again, too hard. Feeling desperate, I scan a first-level book and, with resignation, replace it. With shoulders drooping, I shuffle to the pre-school area. I end up with a gigantic picture book titled *Il Lupo! Il*

Lupo! (The Wolf! The Wolf!)

The book, like the majority of the books in this library, is dog-eared and probably older than I am – more than half a century. I spread its over-sized pages open on a table and, while seated, read it with an Italian/English dictionary in one hand and pen in the other, jotting down new words on a piece of paper. Needing to use a dictionary to read a fairy tale annoys me no end. Since I studied Italian an hour daily in the year before coming to Italy, I thought I would at least be at first-grade level!

The fairy tale *Il Lupo* opens my eyes however. To summarize this *c'era una volta* (once upon a time) story, whenever little Luigi doesn't want to do something, such as take a bath or practice his violin, some adult yells, "The wolf! The wolf!" The oft-repeated threat that the wolf will come if he doesn't obey, always makes Luigi shape up *pronto*.

One day Luigi is walking along a country road when the wolf lunges out of a bush. Fortunately, Luigi out-runs the wolf into town. Scampering around the village, Luigi warns everyone, "The Wolf! The Wolf! The Wolf is coming!" Everyone laughs at him, calls him a jokester.

Meanwhile, the wolf notices that no one believes Luigi so the wolf commences to eat everyone in the village, saving Luigi for dessert. The last page shows a picture of the wolf lounging in bed, licking his claws. A plate of Luigi's bones sits on the wolf's bed stand.

In shock, I stare at the picture on the last page. I don't remember reading a book as violent as this since I was … well … around four years old! The experience of reading this dreadful story as an adult certainly sheds light on why I was such an anxiety-ridden child. I'm sure all such storybooks have since been pitched out of U.S. libraries. If such a book were in the library where I work, the young mothers would scream bloody murder until staff purged it from the collection. Although I'm anti-censorship, I decide it's a good thing our fairy tales are gentler these days.

Despite the violent storybooks and the language barrier, I still love going to the library in Città di Castello, if for no other reason than to read the newspaper. The most charming thing about it is that it seems to be aware that we are living in the 21st century (i.e., it has two visible computers) but, at the same time, continues to function in the ways of the 1950s. No security gate beeps if you accidentally leave without checking out a book. Checking items in and out is still done by hand. There's no barcode scanner, no due-date stampers (amazing, considering the Italians' penchant for stamping documents). There are no videos, CDs, DVDs or CD-ROMs to borrow. To my mind, though, its funky fifties procedures and furniture coupled with its dab of modernity makes it all the more charming. Oh! Did I say ... it's also heated? ♥

7

A TYPICAL DAY

Friends back home e-mail us and ask what we do all day. Since we are not employed and living in Italy, one could easily deduce that all we do is *vacation*. The reality, however, is that everything – from washing clothes to eating dinner – takes longer in Italy.

As soon as my feet hit the floor in the morning, I put a load of clothes into the washing machine. My motto is, "The early bird gets to wear clean and dry clothing." A long timeline stands between dirty-clothes basket and dresser drawer.

First, the capacity of clothes washers in Italy is miniscule.

Second, the wash cycle of these front-loading, purportedly energy-efficient, machines takes, oh, about two hours. Did I mention this was the shortest cycle? Once the machine fills with water, the drum spins ten times clockwise, stops, rests, then spins ten times counter-clockwise, stops and rests. Repeat a gazillion times.

The first time I washed clothes in Giuseppe's machine, I thought it was broken. An hour after putting a load in, I went to the basement to check on it. It was spinning. Back in the apartment, I forgot about it for another hour and when I returned, the machine must have been in rest mode, for when I opened it the clothes I pulled out dripped all over the floor. Having stopped the cycle to open the door meant I had to start the cycle from the beginning. The three words that describe my life in Italy are "trial and error."

Third, clothes dryers are only used by the wealthy. Energy is expensive in Italy, at least twice as expensive as in the U.S. Fortunately, I've always enjoyed hanging clothes outside. The Italian tradition of drying clothes naturally is one of my

Snow gathers on top of our clothes hanging out to dry.

favorites, pulling back memories of childhood, slipping into cool, fresh-smelling sheets on warm summer nights. Until now, I'd never given much thought as to what my mother did during the winter when she had the not-so-glorious task of hanging everything in the basement. Not many people in Italy have basements, so no matter what season it is, people still hang clothes outdoors.

We are advised that cars make excellent dryers when the sun is shining. Simply spread the wet laundry across the seats, dashboard and steering wheel and before you know it, the clothes are dry. If the sun is not shining, a rainforest forms inside the vehicle. We don't have a car so all we can do is dream about this method of drying laundry.

In the old mansion there is a spot for drying wash outdoors. It is accessed from the landing between the first and second floors, á la mezzanine. French doors open onto a cement balcony at the back of the house. A metal railing surrounds the balcony. Beyond the railing two ropes, affixed to metal outcroppings, stretch parallel to the house. Whenever I lean over to hang clothes, I remind myself not look down; it is so high that a bread truck could be parked below and the sheets still wouldn't need to be doubled.

This winter has been unusually snowy and sleety, so quite often I am forced to bring the wet clothes in after they've hung outside for four or five days. I tell Rich jokingly that Frances Mayes may have written *Under the Tuscan Sun*, but I plan to write *Under the Umbrian Clouds*.

We are fortunate that our bathroom has heated towel bars attached to one wall. This expedites drying time considerably, especially for thick socks. Still, drying space is limited. Every radiator in the house usually has some piece of clothing draped over it.

While the clothes spin indefinitely in the washer or hang indefinitely on the line, we have time to run an errand or two. Buying something as simple as a laundry basket, though, means more than a short road trip to K-Mart or Target any day of the week. No American-style chain stores or fast-food franchises can be found in or around Città di Castello, so we must wait until Thursday or Saturday morning when the outdoor market comes to town.

On market days, residents come out in droves. They shop for food, clothes and household items. I suspect that the overriding reason for going to market, though, is to see who's there and to be seen. People run into friends, give them the two-cheeked kiss, and chat awhile, causing others to shoulder around them through the throng until they run across a friend. This all-morning ritual is often followed by a snack of freshly sliced pork on bread purchased from a vendor. We fall into the rhythm quickly, coming to know enough people to spend market day socializing as much as shopping.

On market day we stop for a cappuccino, sitting at a bistro table inside or outside, depending on the weather, taking time to watch the street scene. All manner of people pedal old rusty bicycles: nuns with their veils fanning out like wings; old women in long fur coats and baggy woolen stockings; young women in high heels whose toes are so pointed they could seriously injure small animals; and wrinkly old men with WWII helmets on their heads and cigarettes dangling from their lips. Young people move through the throng on Vespas.

Every morning, retired men gather in the main piazza, hanging out for hours. If a tiny strip of sun happens to slip between the tall buildings

Vendors set up in the middle of Piazza Matteotti.

on a cold winter morning, the men break out of their huddles and line up side-by-side in the sliver of warmth. Yakking to the fellows on either side of them, this is the only time I see Italians stand in a straight line. Italians simply aren't adept at queuing.

In late afternoon, we'll see them again, this time playing or watching bocce ball on the myriad courts around town. Usually they chip in to buy and share a jug of wine. In nicer weather, we see their wives sitting at nearby tables, playing cards.

The coffee bars in Italy are set up so people can be in and out in less than two minutes or hang around all day. Most people walk in, are greeted, place their order, kick back their espresso in one swig while standing at the bar, pay and leave. In the afternoon a lot of customers, elderly women included, ask the barista to add a nip to their espresso, or take a glass of Vinsanto, a strong, sweet wine. These bars also sell pastries and sandwiches and, in the summer, the Italian ice cream, gelato.

Set out for public perusal at each bar is a copy of the two daily newspapers, *La Nazione* and *Il Corriere*, and a copy of the daily sports paper which is, for some reason, pink. Whether you go to the coffee bar first thing in the morning or late at night, those two copies of newspapers will still be there and they'll still be intact. The one-euro cost for a cappuccino and a free read of the newspaper is the best buy in town.

Buying pork sandwiches from a vendor on market day.

The next thing "to do" is to visit the Internet Point – the less expensive, unheated one we refer to as the Cold Place. Neither of the two Internet places has a name, as is often the case for most retail establishments.

Retired men gathering in the main piazza.

Once in awhile I treat myself and patronize the heated Internet Point which costs twice as much per hour. The "Warm Place" keeps the same hours as most shops in small-town Italy, so it is essential to finish before the one p.m. closing.

The three-hour Italian lunch break is necessary to allow time for eating their largest meal of the day, making love and napping. Fortunately for us, with our Type A personalities who always feel out of step and alone between one and four in the afternoon, the Cold Place opens at 8 a.m. and doesn't close until 11 p.m. Owned and operated by Zafer (see photo), from Pakistan, the place even stays open on Christian holidays, such as Easter,

and national holidays. The Cold Place saves us from long, boring afternoons until we learn that we, too, can eat, drink, and make love and nap in the afternoon.

Paying bills while living in a foreign country drains time too. The six-hour time difference between Italy and Eastern Standard Time in the U.S. complicates my Internet bill-paying attempts. I'll often be trying to pay a bill during low-usage hours in America when companies customarily shut down their Web sites for maintenance.

Zafer, owner of the cold place.

This requires me to return to a site repeatedly, sometimes later in the day, until the transaction can be made. On a home computer, you can bookmark those you frequently visit. You can't do that at an Internet Point because you never know which of the dozen computers you'll get. That means "Googling" the company's site every time you want to go to a particular Web page. I'd write down the sites' addresses, but they're so long and convoluted it's simpler to search for them instead. To complicate matters further, each Web site is laid out differently, sometimes forcing me to spend costly minutes trying to figure out how much my bill is and when it's due.

Rich and I sometimes take turns sharing a computer. Other times we each take one for a full hour to correspond with friends – American and Italian – and for Rich to read what happened the day before in American sports. We both read the news, tapping into online newspapers, magazines, Yahoo and CNN reports.

The Cold Place, usually quiet in the afternoon, bustles with activity once five o'clock rolls around. Young Italian and Middle Eastern men huddle around a computer watching one of their buddies correspond in a live chat room. Periodically, roars of laughter and remarks erupt from these groups. Often someone's computer plays Indian, Pakistani or Moroccan music which I like all right, but it confuses me as to where I am, especially when the bells of the Catholic Church next door are clamoring.

Since the Internet Point also houses a bank of ten telephone booths, there's at least one international caller who thinks she needs to yell to be heard.

In addition, the front door (which is propped open even when it is below freezing outside) abuts a narrow street. When you step into the Internet Point you are literally stepping out of the street and into the building. When traffic backs up, the subsequent honking bellows through the Cold Place, causing everyone to stop what they're doing to clasp their hands over their ears.

At lunchtime, we often get caught up amidst the school children being dismissed for the day. Schools start at eight or nine in the morning and end at one p.m. This setup supports the tradition of the entire family sharing at least one meal a day. Although students do not return to school after lunch, they do go to school on Saturdays. Children are required to attend school until age fourteen; after which they can either go to work or attend a specialized secondary school. There are vocational, agricultural, technical and college-prep schools from which to choose.

The stores, reopened after the three-hour afternoon break, brighten the streetscape. Since young people can't get a driver's license until they are eighteen, they tend to spend their evenings hanging out within the ancient walls of the historic center. At the same time, adults are out and about taking their before supper *passeggiatta* – a stroll so slow we have yet to imitate it. Teens in-line skate down cement steps and, despite the cobblestones, toddlers practice walking and children practice riding two-wheeled bicycles. Others run around playing street games while dogs chase after them pell-mell.

Considering the town and its surrounding area is home to 37,000 people, it is safe to say that most people stay home in the evenings. Still, regardless of the weather, the historic center is always crowded enough to bring zest and energy after dark. Whenever we eat out at one of the multitude of restaurants, we bask in that energy and wax poetic about the advantages of a town square.

Our other activities include attending Italian lessons two mornings a week and, in the evenings, practicing Italian, either at the kitchen table with pen and paper or in front of the computer using a CD-ROM. Nearly every night we watch the news and an Italian game show on TV.

Before we left the States, I filled my i-Pod with music and several audio books. We've been in Italy for more than two months and I have yet to listen to any of them. I also brought a dozen embroidery projects and, I've finished, more or less, fifteen stitches in one color. Originally, I'd planned to take a walk every morning, but with all the walking we do just to get through the day, I don't often have the ambition for it. Occasionally, though, especially on Sunday afternoons, Rich and I walk the pretty path alongside the Tiber River which flows to Rome. We've been told the path continues for many miles in both directions and I vow to bike it once the weather improves. Little do I know how significant this footpath will become later in our stay.

A typical day is filled with the host of things everyone needs to do to stay clean and fed. Despite the appearance of typical days, though, not one feels ordinary. Living in a beautiful valley surrounded by snow-capped mountains and Renaissance architecture, and experiencing traditions different from our own, is anything but ordinary. ♡

8

THE POST OFFICE

Before we left for Italy, we sent six boxes addressed to Giuseppe's mansion, one of which we paid extra to go "first class" by air, and the others to go less expensively by sea. The first-class box contains things we want to have fairly quickly – measuring cups and spoons in both metric and American, our favorite Italian cookbooks, the first-aid kit with an assortment of remedies for minor maladies and, most importantly, our prescription medicines for the year. The remaining boxes, the ones coming by boat, contain our clothes for spring and summer and travel books we'll need later in the year. Because we left in January, we figured we could wait the four to six weeks for their arrival and, by enduring the wait, save hundreds of dollars in postal costs.

Now that we are living in an apartment in Giuseppe's mansion, we wonder how the boxes will come to us. This is not a private residence as we'd first believed. Giuseppe's older sister lives in an apartment on the first floor, and a family with two teenagers and a dog live on the third. Will our boxes be left outside on the common doorstep? What if it's raining the day they're delivered? Surely, we can't expect any of the other residents to haul them inside.

Wonder turns to worry when, looking down from our balcony one day, I spy the postal carrier drive up to the wrought-iron gate on a motorcycle. He wears a helmet, a cigarette dangles from his mouth, and he sits astride, toe tips touching the ground as he sorts through a stack of envelopes. The sight of him raises the same question I had as a child about the tiny sleigh Santa Claus drove. How in heaven's name could he fit everything, including large packages, in that one small vehicle?

A few days later, we find a tiny slip of paper under the common door of the four-apartment manse. It is from the post office and addressed to us.

Standing outside on the stoop, we peer at the piece of paper. We guess the post office tried to deliver the first-class box earlier but we weren't home to receive it. Now what? After we both read the instructions on the slip of paper five times, we conclude we have no idea what it says. Looking into Rich's eyes, which mirror the trepidation I feel, we know there is no choice but to go to the post office.

Thankfully, Giuseppe had taken us there as part of our tour of the area, so it wasn't as if we didn't know how to get inside the building. To enter, one has to stand in front of a narrow glass door which, after what seems like an eternity, slowly slides open. You step into a glass compartment which can accommodate two people comfortably. If a third person happens to squeeze in, all the postal clerks lift their heads in unison and shout, "Only two at a time!" It's as though they have eyes on the sides of their faces, like fish. Once the door behind you shuts, which takes a long time even when a stranger has not jumped in with you, the door in front of you opens and you step into the post office.

The post office.

We're told the reason for this setup, both at the post office and at banks, is to discourage robbers. Post offices in Italy not only handle the nation's mail, but also are a repository for paying utility bills and for the dispensing of pension checks. Since Italians use cash for nearly every transaction, the post office is, on any given day, chock-full of euros.

Once inside, people take turns as they would in a bakery or a meat market – by pulling a number. In this case, the number comes out of a large chartreuse and blue machine, the post office colors. The only problem is that there are four different buttons, each, I assume, corresponding to a different teller. There are words next to each button, but none make any sense to me. Looking over my shoulder, I see that each teller has a number displayed digitally above their window. The numbers indicate which customer is being waited on at the moment. My extensive experience in trial-and-error during high school algebra prepared me well for functioning in an Italian post office. And, since Giuseppe had already taken us here, I have an inkling as to which window I want to go to; the mailing window versus the pension check or utility bill windows. The "mailing" clerk is currently waiting on #45. What I don't know is which of the four choices on the ticket machine will give me a ticket to that window.

I poke the top button, and pull out a slip of paper that says #20. Not even close to #45. I punch the second button – out comes #112. Hitting the third button, the machine spits out #47. This could be the one. The last button produces #80. Five people hover in the area in front of the window that is serving #20. I say "hover" because Italians do not line up properly. They form globs instead of lines.

I quickly learn that it is not uncommon while standing in line to watch your number come and go on the overhead monitor while you continue to wait behind people who obviously arrived before you. Pardon me for saying this, but the postal clerks in Italy appear to be trigger happy. They forward the digital number machine while a customer is in front of them, and then forward it again after the customer leaves.

A half hour later, Rich and I finally step in front of a clerk. We're standing ankle deep in the slips of paper others have pulled from the machine. I notice a few slips of paper in the waste basket next to me, and a few others clinging for life on the edge of the counter. These piles of litter on the floor, reminiscent of fallen tree leaves in autumn, surprise me because I've never seen an Italian throw litter on the ground outside. In fact, I've seen, on many occasions, *teenage* Italians walk across a street to dispose of their litter properly.

Restraining myself from pushing the cliff-hanging slips off the counter to the floor, I show the clerk the paper regarding the delivery of our box. She explains something to us in Italian. She can tell by looking at our faces that we didn't understand a word she said. She summons another clerk, who says something to us and finally a third one joins who repeats the second, only a bit louder. We still stare back at them dumbstruck. At long last everyone understands we don't understand and will never understand no matter how many times they repeat themselves.

Suddenly we hear someone speaking English – English with a British accent. A squat elderly woman, spectacles covering her brown prairie-dog eyes, gently pulls us aside.

"May I introduce myself," she says in that polite way Britons have. "I'm Mrs. Parker. Can I be of service to you?"

Rich and I both sigh. We are sinking fast here in the post office and in desperate need of rescue. We relay the situation to her and hand her the notice we received. Taking it in with one glance, she raises her head and in a loud voice she calls to the clerk and translates the problem into lovely, sprightly and commanding Italian.

Turning to us, she says, "They don't have the box here. You must call the number on this slip of paper." My heart sinks but before it hits bottom, Mrs. Parker whips out a cell phone from her coat pocket and, while flipping it open with one hand, asks if we want her to make the call. Our heads bob vigorously. We had started to feel a dire yearning for some of the things in the box, saying on numerous occasions how this or that problem would be solved once that box arrived. Rich especially wanted the shoes he liked to wear while working out at the gym, and I was hankering for the paperbacks I'd packed.

Mrs. Parker places the call and after ten minutes of speaking Italian into the phone, not a word of which we understand despite our studies, she flips it shut and slides it into her pocket, hands the slip of paper to us and says the box will be delivered the next day.

"Be sure to be home to receive it," she warns, "otherwise it will be sent to Perugia." Perugia is the capital of the province of Umbria, and is over fifty miles away.

We thank her profusely and exchange cell phone numbers. By the time we make it out of the double doors onto the street, Mrs. Parker is already astride her bicycle.

"By the way," she says, "Where are you from?"

"America," I say.

As she pushes off on her bicycle she calls over her shoulder, "Oh, I'm so sorry, dear. There is nothing I can do about that."

We chuckle, amazed at how such a small body can contain both an imp and an angel.

At eleven o'clock the next day, after watching the postal employee on the motorcycle come and go, I sit on the couch and fret. I should know better. Fretting is such a waste of time. Five hours later, when the sun has given up the day and we have given up hope of a delivery, the doorbell rings. I fly down the flights of stairs like a teenager about to meet her boyfriend. Flinging the door open wide I stretch my arms out for the first-class box which a delivery man rests awkwardly on his knee. As he dumps the box into my arms I glance beyond the man's shoulder to the curb where he has parked an extremely small white truck. I decide both he and Santa are miracle workers.

Upstairs, as though it's Christmas, Rich and I tear into the box and pull out its contents. Twenty seconds later we stare speechless at the things spread around us. Other than our prescription medicines, what on earth had we thought so important about the contents of this box? Not even Rich's gym shoes or my paperback novels were inside. Sitting back on our heels, we recall all we'd thought we had packed in the carton. It soon becomes apparent that the box would have needed to be large enough to house a refrigerator to accommodate our imaginings.

~~~

Every day after that, whenever we return home, we look carefully for possible notices from the post office under the door and around the front stoop. The remaining five boxes are supposed to arrive four to six weeks after mailing. We are at the seven-week mark. The temperatures outside are rising and our spring and summer clothes are in those boxes. Friends joke that we can always go day tripping to Milan to buy new ones, and as fun as that sounds, we are on a strict budget. Besides, I know I'll be more comfortable with the clothes I'd sent.

While watching the news on TV one evening, our worry devolves into nervous banter. The video clip shows a group of Italian men standing around a bunch of cardboard boxes piled on a dock. They keep pointing at them and talking about them. In our vulnerable place of illiteracy, we joke that they are saying, "If the people who own these boxes don't come and pick them up we're going to shove them into the ocean." My laughter turns to sober silence. I'm more attached to stuff than I imagined.

Once again we set out for the post office, this time with our U.S. receipts in hand. Post office staffers stare at our receipts and shake their heads. English is as incomprehensible to them as Italian is to us. Once again no one has any idea where the boxes are, but they all agree they aren't in the post office. We don't want to bother Mrs. Parker, for by now we know her husband is handicapped and we are concerned he needs her more than we do.

I tell Rich not to worry about the boxes because before we mailed them, I'd performed an act of genius. I had printed Giuseppe's permanent residence in Bologna for the return address. If the boxes don't come to the mansion in Città di Castello, they'll go to Giuseppe's other address in Bologna – not our home address in Michigan. Giuseppe often comes to visit his sister and friends in Città di Castello, and if the boxes happen to be delivered to Bologna, surely he'd bring them to us.

Giuseppe does come to Città di Castello and drops by one day, but not with any boxes. Rich is out biking with his Italian buddies, all of whom are happily pedaling up the surrounding Apennine Mountains. Once in Italian class I referred to this group of cyclists as the *ascensori* (ascensionists), and our Italian teacher corrected me, saying only Jesus Christ can ascend. But that's a whole other story.

I make espressos, as Giuseppe had taught me, and we sit and sip them. I tell him the sad story of our delinquent boxes. He asks if I have receipts, and when I show them to him, he says, "Come on. Let's go to the post office." He gulps his espresso in one swallow and we're off.

I am thrilled. This time I'm going to the post office without an ounce of trepidation. Giuseppe can get anything done. He's lived in this town almost seventy years, he knows what's what, and he knows how to get things done without being abrasive. Plus, Italian is his mother tongue.

He talks to the clerks for at least twenty minutes. How much can be said in that amount of time? I begin to surmise that Italians take a lot longer to say things than we do. While I'm trying to imagine what they're saying, he abruptly stops talking, waves to me to follow him and we return to his car. He drives about two blocks away to what looks to be an apartment building. We get out of the car and walk up to the door. He rings the buzzer, holding his ear close to the speaker since the traffic is noisy. No one comes to the door, but a woman standing on an abundantly flowered balcony above us calls down. "No one is there." Giuseppe drives me back to the apartment and says we'll have to wait until after lunch – four p.m.

After five o'clock, while Rich is still out biking, the doorbell rings. Once again, I fly down the stairs to open it. Giuseppe stands there with a crooked grin on his face. I invite him in, but instead he gives me the Italian hand signal to follow him. Out on the gravel driveway my knees go weak and I nearly faint. Stuffed in his little silver car are our boxes, pressed up hard against the windows. How he got them all in there I'll never know. Surely we'll need the Jaws of Life to extract them. Squealing with delight, I run to help him carry the boxes upstairs. He waves me off. "You go up," he instructs. You might think it is my squealing that spurs him on to bring the boxes up without my assistance, but I assure you it is because my helping would have been an affront to his virility. It's a macho thing that continues to flourish here and, independent cuss that I am, a difficult one for me to get used to.

Five trips that man makes back and forth – from the car to our second-floor apartment. When he gently sets the last one down, he dances a little jig and points a tah-dah! with both arms extended toward the boxes. He beams. I hold my hands to my face and cry tears of relief. I run to him and give him a big hug and cheek kisses.

After I calm down a bit, I ask Giuseppe where he'd found them. Three of the boxes, he says, had been in the garage of that house we'd gone to earlier. For the other two he had to drive fifty miles to the main post office in Perugia, and fifty miles back again. I can't believe it. And I can't wait for Rich to get home to see. ♥

9

FROM CITY TO COUNTRY

It's the end of February and Giuseppe's kind offer to get us started has expired. He needs his apartment, so we must find another place to live. This means having to deal with yet another kind of establishment – a real estate office.

The fact that the real estate agencies do not list all their offerings cooperatively in one newspaper, magazine or Web site is a handicap for those of us without a car. Additional hindrances include not having enough language skills to simply phone the various agencies; we have to walk to each one.

Being foreigners in a non-touristy town, plus looking to rent instead of buy, doesn't get agents jumping out of their chairs to help us either. Another drawback is that Italians don't value making money the way Americans do. I have to stop myself from viewing an agent's lack of follow-up as laziness and remind myself of the Italians' priorities: eating well, socializing and family. No wonder Italy can be both relaxing and frustrating at the same time.

After much tramping around and getting rejected, we meet two nice young women from two separate agencies on opposite sides of town. Lucia is a slim fresh-faced young woman in her late twenties, with nicely highlighted brown hair, bright brown eyes and a tiny diamond pierced in the side of her nose. She looks and acts hip, knows a lot of English and, as a town native, knows the place and its people inside out.

It's significant that we meet Lucia today because I know that if I were to review my hair over the past five weeks, it looks its very best at this moment. This means that tomorrow it will be in urgent need of a cut. Lucia seems like the perfect person to ask for a hair stylist recommendation. Before even looking for possible apartment rentals, she puts earning money aside and makes an appointment for the next day with her friend Andrea. The salon's business card she hands me reads, "A & W, Andrea and Wally."

The next morning, when I walk into the third-floor salon, a beautiful dark-haired 30-something woman stops sweeping the highly polished wood floor and greets me. After we establish that I am Lucia's "friend," she puts the broom away, seats me at the wash bowl and swishes a cape around me. She speaks extremely loud, so loud I can't make out much of what she's saying. All I catch is that her husband will be right back; he's gone outside for a cigarette.

Since I'm only tilted back a few inches, water runs into my ears, further impeding any chance of my understanding her. From this view, though, I admire the salon's high-ceilinged wood beams, stained a deep blonde. A wall of windows looks out over the tops of pine trees. Thoughtfully placed mirrors and track lighting, and glass tables decorated with large vases of silk flowers create a spa-like atmosphere.

You can imagine my surprise when the woman's husband returns and introduces himself as Andrea (pronounced ahn-DRAY-ah ... not ANN-dree-ah), as in Andrea Bocelli, and that Wally (pronounced VAH-lee not WAL-lee) is the woman washing my hair!

Andrea, who shaves his head bald like just about every other man in Italy, is the kind of man who, like just about every other man in Italy, loves women, regardless of their age. Nearly every man I meet here makes me feel like a schoolgirl. It doesn't matter if he is my age, half my age, or twice my age – every one of them flirts with me. Not with pinches, thank goodness, but with their eyes – eyes that either twinkle or wink. One handsome twenty-something actually had the cheek to surreptitiously wink at me while Rich and I walked hand in hand.

The bottom line is: Andrea wants me to look "younger and sexier" – his words, in English, no kidding. He doesn't say "young and sexy," he says, "youngER and sexiER." In the mirror I watch a man in a state of joy while coloring my hair blonde (I'm a brunette) and cutting it short and sassy. I suspect it thrills him to

Wally and Andrea with their son.

use a color other than red, the preferred dark-haired Italian woman's choice for a change from black. An hour later, when I leave the shop, I do feel younger and sexier.

That evening, Lucia (who is as excited as I am with my new cut) walks Rich and me to see two apartments inside the city's walls. Neither one, though, has an outdoor eating area which, we now realize, is a must-have. Besides needing two bedrooms (one for guests we expect to host from the U.S.), and a reasonable monthly rental cost, everything else is negotiable. We neither need nor can afford anything fancy.

Since Lucia has only two apartments to show, we have to go to another real estate office to see more. We get lucky at an agency near the Cold Internet Place where we are greeted by Federica, another young woman in her twenties. She wears a visible layer of foundation, has perfectly straight dyed-black shoulder-length hair and bangs and doesn't speak a word of English. She tells us she has a couple apartments out in the country. Would we like to see them?

The country – now that sounds really good, especially with spring right around the corner. Federica makes arrangements for us to visit them and brings along her colleague, Monica, who speaks some English.

Once the four of us walk out of the office onto the cobblestone street, both women stop and turn to us. Their faces are questioning. We ask, "What's wrong?" Monica says, in English, "Where is your car?" We say we don't have a car. Their jaws drop. It is assumed, I suspect, that all Americans have a car. I would not have blamed them if they backed out on the spot. After all, we can't speak Italian; we want to rent, not buy; and not having a car means one of them will have to use her own precious petrol to drive us around the countryside. To their credit, they follow through with us anyhow.

Without a car, we realize now, we have yet another requirement – the place either has to have bus service or be within walking distance of town, preferably both. Both places we see have beautiful views and are the right price, but they're out in the boondocks. It's miles to the closest bus stop and grocery store. When we return to their office, while discussing other possibilities, a priest enters. The young women immediately stand, put their hands in prayer position and bow their heads. Rich and I exchange a glance and follow suit. Without introduction or explanation, the priest sprinkles water over all of us in a Lenten blessing and then leaves to go on to the next business. Immediately, we re-seat ourselves and continue our discussion as though there'd been no interruption.

It takes several "dates" with both agencies before Federica finds an apartment in the country, a mere three miles (five kilometers) from town. As soon as we see it, we take it.

The following Sunday, Quinto drives over and helps us put all our stuff in his car and drives us to our new place. I don't even want to think of how we would have managed without him.

Formerly a farmhouse, Macrì Country House was renovated five years earlier into six apartments. It is owned by dapper Domenico and operated by his wife, Lucia, both in their fifties. The property includes a built-in swimming pool (which will cost extra in the summer, but well worth it to us), and a restaurant across the gravel parking lot where their beautiful daughter Maria is the cook. Amidst the acres of "back yard," which Lucia says we're free to roam, is an empty horse corral, hills and a path that winds up to a grape vineyard, orchard and forest, and a large pond where

Macrì Country House.

guests can fish. All this is situated in a valley of meadows and farmland surrounded by the Apennine Mountains.

The apartment, on the second floor, has two large bedrooms furnished with heavy antique furniture. Like the dressers and bed stands at Giuseppe's apartment, these too are topped with a slab of gray marble. Its third room, a combination kitchen/dining room/living room, is known in Italy as an *angolo cotura*. The old-fashioned tradition of having the three rooms combined reminds me of today's "Great Room" concept and the adage, "The more things change, the more they stay the same."

The ceilings in all three rooms are high, made of brick and shored up by heavy wood beams. The walls are white stucco and the floors tiled with smooth, non-porous bricks. The centerpiece of the Great Room is a heavy farm table made of dark wood, surrounded by four straight-back cane chairs and a long wooden bench. Behind the table is the kitchen counter (all two feet of it), topped with gray marble, and stainless steel sink. Instead of cupboards underneath the counter, the space is skirted with a cheerful red, yellow and orange plaid fabric. The refrigerator stands as high as the kitchen counter. There is only one cupboard – a drying cupboard for dishes like the one we had in the first apartment. A wood hutch will have to serve extra duty as cupboard for extra dishes, pots, pans and canned goods. A 14-inch color TV sits precariously on a small cabinet. Despite connecting to cable, it doesn't offer any channels in English.

The four-burner stove is so tiny I refer to it as a "Barbie" stove. Underneath the stove-top, hidden by a little ceramic door, is empty space – not even a hint of an oven. The "oven" is the *forno*, as the Italians call an oven, located outside. It will serve as our grill as well.

Lucia says we can either buy wood to burn in the *forno* or gather it from around the property. We choose gathering wood. After all, we aren't millionaires and, besides, as a lifetime Girl Scout who still takes the word "thrifty" to heart, I can't resist the thrill of gathering our own wood and saving money at the same time.

Lucia, about the same age, height and weight as I am, spends her time greeting guests in her easy-going way, scheduling their stays, ensuring the apartments are cleaned, food ordered and prepared for the on-site restaurant, and the property is kept trim and in order. We can't communicate because of the language barrier; still, she manages to tell me

L'angola cotura includes the living/dining room and kitchen.

The "Barbie" stove is tucked to the left of the sink and counter.

she thinks I am thin. She holds up her pinky and gently shakes it at me while pointing at me with the other hand. I like her so much!

Despite our inability to communicate fully, she welcomes us warmly by giving us a sack of fresh oranges from Calabria (a treat in mid-March), an Italian sausage and a used, three-piece sectional couch for our apartment. Rich and I buy colorful orange/red/yellow plaid bed sheets to drape over the couch that has seen better days. The orangey skirt covering the area under the sink set the color theme and we run with it.

At Rich's request, Lucia has her handyman, Paolo, put in a skylight that can be opened and shut in the formerly windowless, airless, claustrophobic bathroom. When we tell her we'll be eating outside a lot, she provides us with an outdoor table and two chairs. When I ask where I can hang our laundry she gives me a white-enameled drying rack for underwear and socks and has Paolo string three parallel ropes between two trees in the yard for our larger items. When I ask her if she has a small table for my computer, Paolo delivers a bamboo one and a matching chair with a cushion. Have I mentioned how much I like this woman?

We can live without an oven, freezer, dishwasher, disposal, and microwave and, with summer coming, I'm happy with the shower-only, no-tub bathroom. Lighting the stove burners with a long candle lighter before each use is easier than using a match as we had to do when I was growing up.

What we desperately need, though, is a washing machine. Without a car, there is no way we can lug our laundry to and from town; besides, there are no Laundromats, and the drop-off and pickup laundries charge more than our budget will allow. With Lucia's blessing, we purchase a washing machine and have it installed under the kitchen counter, hidden by the plaid skirt. We figure it will be a nice parting gift to Lucia when we return to the States.

We can't afford fancy, and fancy we do not get. But we get so much more instead. The views from all three of our windows are like postcards, the people who own and take care of the property are kind, and we have an unimaginable luxury – a built-in swimming pool for hot summer days. A bus stop on the highway is down the dirt road, about a "block" away. In two days we'll need to be at our Italian lesson by 9:30 a.m. Now, all we (actually Rich) have to do is figure out the bus schedule. My top priority becomes finding a way to walk to town. ♥

The pool at Macrí.

1 0

POST OFFICE REDUX

The first few times going in and out of the post office via the Plexiglas compartment seemed strange, but familiarity breeds acceptance. That seems to be the Italian way – acceptance always trumps contempt, thus the reason for the patience Italians continually display. I cling to this thought as I watch the seated post office clerk working on the five envelopes I want sent to the U.S. As she slaps an air mail sticker on each one, I think a preschooler could do this. Why doesn't she simply hand me all the stamps and air mail stickers and have me ready the envelopes myself? Being some thirty years her senior, I know I've slapped more stamps on envelopes than she has.

Still not finished, she struggles to open a glue stick, which she rubs across the back of a stamp. After she places it on an envelope, she stands and, with the palm of her hand, presses the stamp with so much force one foot leaves the floor.

A gaggle of people wait behind me. Glancing over my shoulder, I don't notice anyone rolling their eyes, or murmuring under their breath. In fact, their faces are placid, their bodies relaxed.

I pay and receive my change and am about to take leave when the clerk starts a pleasant conversation. *È questa la sua prima volta in Italia?* (Is this your first visit to Italy?) *Come Le piace?* (How are you liking it?) *Sarà qui quante settimane?* (How many weeks will you be here?) Having thought the transaction finished, my mind has relaxed and is no longer on "Italian

Speaking" alert. I blurt a few words and she seems pleased enough.

⁓⁂⁓

Another day I go to the post office to send a birthday present to
Chicago. To the postal clerk I proffer a sturdy box – one I'd found outside
a retail shop waiting to be picked up by the trash collector – into which I'd
lovingly packed our daughter Chelsea's new Italian leather purse. The clerk
tells me the box is too big for her scale. She demonstrates, not once, but
twice, its largeness. Each time she tries to balance the box on the tiny scale
it falls off. I ask what I should do and she speaks to me as if she were the
dreaded "Soup Nazi" on *Jerry Seinfeld*. Since I don't understand a word of
her response, I take the box back and walk cautiously to the exit because
at this moment there'd be nothing more humiliating than slipping on the
pieces of paper littering the floor. Not only would I have to endure the fall,
but everyone inside the post office would have extra time to stare at me
while I stood in the glass compartment waiting to exit.

With new resolve the next day, I return and get a very nice gentleman
who not only speaks some English, but also doesn't mind getting up from
his chair to walk over to a larger scale.

The following month, when it is time to send my daughter-in-law, Hai
Yan, a birthday present, I can't find a free box waiting to be picked up by
the garbage collector, so I break down and buy one at the post office. I'd
bought Hai Yan a bag of Perugian chocolates, and a small bottle of perfume
from a *profumeria*. Hai Yan, continues to wait for her visa while living with
our son in China. The postage to China will be huge. The very nice postal
worker – the one who got off his chair to use a larger scale – weighs the
package and shakes his head. Again, standing up, he turns a three-ring
binder around so I can see it. He points to a figure which makes my eyes go
round. In a hushed voice he suggests I either go to Mail Boxes, Etc. – near
the railroad station – or remove the bag of candy to lighten the load and
thus make it less expensive to send. I don't have the heart to remove the
candy, so I tromp over to Mail Boxes, the present still housed in the blue-

and-chartreuse post office box I'd purchased.

The young woman at Mail Boxes, Etc. barely acknowledges me, which is unusual in Italy. She wants to know what is in the box. When I tell her chocolates, she says the company cannot possibly send food. (I always knew chocolate was real food.) She asks if anything else is in it and I tell her about the perfume. She places a phone call, asks about the perfume, and returns the receiver to its cradle. She quickly turns toward me and says, no, the perfume can't be sent either. It could start a fire. Ai, yi, yi!

I return to the post office and, as luck would have it, get the "small-scale" clerk again. I don't want to pay for more than 1.5 kilos (listen to me, sounding like a drug dealer) because the rate would have cost more than the gift. The "small-scale" clerk notes with disdain that the box has not been taped. I say I am sorry and hang my head. How many times have I silently scolded people in front of me in line at the U.S. post office for not having taped their boxes before leaving home? The clerk reaches for a roll of tape but before she can do anything I ask her to weigh the package first. She makes a face, but does as I ask. Just over 1.5 kilos. I rip open the bag of chocolates, take a handful of the wrapped candies out, place them in front of her and say, *"Per Lei,"* dump the rest loosely into the gift bag which holds the hermetically sealed perfume and ask her to weigh it again. Still too heavy. I take out a few more candies and gently push them in her direction. Her face softens. She weighs the box again. Perfect, just under 1.5 kilos.

She proceeds to tape the box, which I think is very nice. The strange thing about it is that she doesn't have either a tape dispenser or a pair of scissors, forcing her to tear off pieces with her teeth. Once, during her struggle, the entire roll falls into her lap, taping itself to itself. No wonder she's always in a bad mood. Who wouldn't be while doing the work the customer should have done before leaving home and, on top of that, her employer failing to provide the equipment necessary to do a proper job? I should have given her a tape dispenser, not a handful of chocolates.

By the time I step into the glass compartment waiting to exit the post office, I notice she has disappeared, along with the chocolates. I smile, happy I could bring a little joy into her life. That's the emotion I equate with chocolate. 💕

Update: *Not only does Hai Yan receive her birthday present in China, everything we send from the Italian post office throughout the year arrives safely and in a timely manner.*

Update to robbers: *In the summertime, I walk past the post office and notice the set of double doors are propped wide open, probably to let air in.*

11

EASTER

GOOD FRIDAY

Having become accustomed to the town's eight sets of bells tolling the hours, half hours and quarter hours, and clanging discordantly whenever summoning congregants to mass, our experience of Good Friday begins with their silence. That change, by itself, sets the tone for the evening ceremony, which begins at nine, long after the sun has set and the air turns nippy.

All the street, store and house lights are doused before the Good Friday procession begins. The only light comes from the torches carried by participants, and a full moon. Even before the procession reaches where we stand on the steps of an old church, we can see in the distance the flickering shadows of torches licking the third and fourth stories of the three-hundred-year-old facades. The sight of everything else, enveloped in darkness, produces a chill down my spine. The dull, repetitive beat of one drum – two slow, four fast – casts a pall of silence over everyone – not a whisper or whimper – only the sound of the drum and our own hearts beating.

Hundreds of residents, dressed in 13th Century costumes, lead the funeral march up and down the narrow streets of Città di Castello. Soldiers, reminiscent of the Crusades, carry swords, shields, spears and staffs. They wear navy blue and red woolen tunics over long-sleeved, loosely woven mesh tops. Medieval monks shrouded in long robes, their heads and faces hooded in brown wool, clutch cumbersome crosses. Some women wear woolen peasant dresses, while others have draped heavy navy capes over finer clothing. Pallbearers lug a pallet with a statue of Jesus lying on it.

Once the torchbearers, clergy, soldiers, peasants, pallbearers and a ragtag band playing a funeral dirge pass us, the spectators fall in behind. They carry candles they'd brought from home. Hundreds of people, from very young to very old, participate. Everyone follows the procession to where it began at the cathedral on the west side of the fortressed city, where the local bishop speaks. Modern loudspeakers transmit his message through the dark.

Afterward the crowd breaks up and the atmosphere abruptly turns joyful. Shouts of *Buona Pasqua* (Happy Easter) fill the night air. Knots of people form, greeting each other with cheek kisses. No one seems in a hurry to leave.

Rich and I walk to a little church nearby where some of the costumed participants have gone to change back into their 21st century attire. They are members of a confraternity whose purpose is to keep the traditions of Christianity alive while acknowledging that Christianity is not the only true way. There, we wait for our friends, Giordano and his wife Clemenza, both members of the confraternity. They had invited us to the procession and kindly offered to drive us home to Macrì afterward. As we wait for them, I stare at the cobblestones and wonder what violence and what joys they'd borne through the centuries.

EASTER SUNDAY

As in other Christian-based cultures, Easter Sunday in Italy begins with morning Mass followed by a huge meal. It can be enjoyed at home or a restaurant, with relatives or friends. In Italy it is said that Christmas is for family and Easter is "free choice."

There is no Easter bunny, but children receive a large chocolate egg, hollow inside so as to hold a gift. The eggs are wrapped in shiny gold, red, or silver-and-blue paper. That is all they get – no baskets filled with jellybeans, spongy chicks or foil-wrapped chocolates.

A traditional cake, called *La Colomba,* is served or given as gifts on Easter. My dictionary translates *colomba* as "pigeon." When we're told the bird symbolize peace, I decide a *colomba* must really be a "dove." Later I learn there is no biological difference between a pigeon and a dove. The difference, like so many other things in life, is how we perceive them: either they are a nuisance when we walk through a park or piazza, or a gentle, avian of peace that floats high above the city.

The cake, *La Colomba,* is a buttery sweet cake with almonds and frosting dribbled on top. We are given one as a gift and it is so large it will take us the entire week to finish it. It is still March and we eat it topped with fresh strawberries from southern Italy.

Under cloudy skies, we walk to town on Easter Sunday since no local buses run on Sunday. With great relish we slowly consume an extraordinary dinner at Luigi and Nadia's restaurant, *Trattoria Il Feudo* (The Feudal). As Luigi explains it, when you dine here, the customers are the royalty and he and Nadia are the slaves.

Luigi kindly seats us next to the radiator. Having lived in Canada, he knows it is difficult for foreigners to get accustomed to dining without heat. Leaning against it relieves me from some of the chill, but still my ankles and feet are freezing. Of course once I start drinking wine, I warm to the tips of my toes.

The dinner includes an *antipasto* of grilled red peppers with melted goat cheese on top served with a honey mustard and olive oil; then hand-made, melt-in-your-mouth lasagna; and lamb, roasted the way it was roasted 900 years ago – in terra cotta. We drink red wine with dinner and, for dessert, enjoy lightly lemon-flavored cake.

After dinner it is customary to order an espresso, which Rich does, but I order my preference – a cappuccino – instead. This forces Luigi, an astute chef, to wring his hands and whisper under his breath. Between gritted teeth he says rapidly, in ultra-enunciated English: "I will bring it only because it is Easter, but this is the last time!" The edict, "Thou shall not have a cappuccino after twelve noon," may as well be written in the Italian government's law books.

The purported reason behind drinking an espresso as opposed to a cappuccino (or a café-latte or macchiato, for that matter) is that it's not good for the digestion to have a drink laced with milk after a large meal – technically the noontime meal in Italy. Nearly every afternoon, however, I buck the "law" and order a cappuccino at one of several coffee bars. I've always been served without wisecrack or disdain, but a glance around confirms I am usually the only one breaking the unwritten law. On occasion, though, I'll catch an old woman sipping a cappuccino after the proscribed hours. Personally, I think old women can do whatever they please.

By the time we finish eating Easter dinner, it is late enough to go to the telephone/internet place to call our relatives in Chicago. The night before, the Italians had switched to daylight savings time (a week before the U.S.), making it an eight-hour time difference between Italy and Chicago instead of the usual seven hours. Thankfully, it will stay light longer now, allowing us to walk home before dark.

EASTER MONDAY

We are surprised to learn that Easter Monday is every bit as much a holiday as Easter. Everything is closed except churches. Not one grocery store is open, and restaurants are typically closed on Mondays anyway. Not having planned ahead for yet another holiday, we would have starved had it not been for dear Quinto and Liana. They invited us to their country house for what we know will not be a chocolate dinner, although I wouldn't have cared if that was the only item on the menu.

For Italians not fortunate enough to have a house in the country, which is the majority of them, the tradition is to go to the country for a picnic. Judging from watching the news that night, Easter Monday is a holiday much like our Memorial Day used to be when it fell on a weekday. Masses of cars creep out of town in the morning and repeat the march in reverse later in the day. Thankfully, the country house we go to is only a ten-minute drive up a mountain from Macrì and Quinto picks us up.

While Quinto and Liana work on the finishing touches of the festive meal to come, they send us off to the far end of their property with two sets of binoculars. The vistas, despite overcast skies, are extraordinary in every direction.

Liana joins us as we're pointing at a car wending its way up the mountain. Leaning over the railing to get a better look, Liana says it's her son's car. He, his wife and their dog will be joining us for the festivities. We are delighted to learn that Tomasso and Veronica speak English well, which makes the day even more of a holiday for us who find prolonged speaking in and listening to Italian hard work.

The festive meal proceeds as tradition dictates, starting with a cold *antipasto* in the form of sandwiches. We eat these outside while sitting on the patio around a bistro table, taking in the scenery. I could have stopped eating after that because a sandwich is all I usually eat for lunch anyway. Liana graciously moves us inside, however, to the already set table. As is her custom whenever we visit, she makes sure Rich and I are the ones seated closest to the fireplace.

The second course, eaten at the table, is the warm *primo*; a delicious lasagna Liana had made and Quinto baked in their outdoor *forno*. The next course, the *secondo*, includes lamb chops and sausage, both cooked over the fire in the fireplace, accompanied by a side dish of marinated artichokes.

After dinner we lounge in front of the blazing fire, switching between Italian and English, until my brain starts to go limp. We sip liqueur, nibble chocolate and fork liqueur-covered cake into our mouths. By and by most of us fall into a food-laden stupor. Quinto, though, unable to bear the inactivity, pulls himself off the couch and goes outside to cut the lawn which, to be honest, needed a trim about as much as indoor-outdoor carpeting needs a trim. Liana, Tomasso, Veronica and I envy his ambition through heavy-lidded eyes. I can tell that Rich, though, who has become accustomed to riding a bicycle up the mountains, envies his activity. ♥

Update: Later in the year Rich will drop in on Liana and Quinto at their country house. His arrival, after scaling the steep hill on his bicycle, will both shock and delight them.

Update: We'll have another dinner there with just the four of us. Afterward, we'll spend the afternoon relaxing on the couch while listening to opera. This is the "sweet life" Italy is known for.

12

FRIENDS

Although the food, scenery, culture and architecture of Italy is as wonderful as advertised, the thing I enjoy most is its people and the friends, both Italian and American, we've made here. In addition to Giuseppe and his wife Nerina, and their friends Quinto and Liana, there are six other people who help keep our social calendar packed.

We met Giordano soon after we arrived, when people were still using umbrellas as shields against the wet golf ball-size snowflakes that fell nearly every morning during the 9:30 "rush" hour in Città di Castello. Rich and I were in the tourist information office asking yet another question to which the answer was, roughly translated, "We are a tourist information center, not a fount of wisdom for new residents." Giordano was posting a notice for one of the many groups to which he belongs. He'd overheard our questions to the weary clerk and struck up a conversation in English.

Rich and Giordano glommed onto the subject of road bicycling as though they were wearing helmets and their bikes were leaning against their hip bones. Giordano, a native Italian, who speaks both English and German fluently, invited Rich to ride bikes with him once the weather turned. We left the office with his phone number. Much to everyone's disappointment, the

Giordano.

nasty weather didn't break for a couple months.

Giordano, who is in his mid-fifties, has an unassuming appearance. If you were introduced to him you'd never guess he is an elite athlete; he stands about 5'6", is balding and his brown eyes are covered by thick glasses. Nor would you get a sense of his ability to galvanize people around his ideas; he has an unpretentious approach that seldom fails to persuade. Despite this description of him, he would be the first to admit he is often in the dog house wherever his beautiful and gracious wife Clemenza is concerned.

What gets him in trouble (and scores him high points in my book) is his obsession with ascending mountains ... on a bicycle. He spends every spare moment doing it. I've heard people refer to him as "fanatical" and "over the top." If he is reading this, you can bet your life savings he is blushing – with pride – in the same way he blushes when he says in English, head bowed, hands resting lightly on a glass of freshly squeezed orange or blackberry juice: "Mya wife, she isa mad atta me." We have become such good friends we can ask in response, "So, what's new, Giordano?"

Giordano's long-suffering wife is Clemenza, a lovely lady who expands our circle of friends.

When Giordano and Rich start hooking up a couple times each week for what I consider to be long rides (50 – 120 miles a day) up tall mountains, I fall to my knees so hard I nearly crack the floor. I thank God a hundred thousand times that I no longer feel obligated to go on bicycle rides with my husband – bicycle rides that weren't all that exciting for him anyway. Not even in my younger days could I bike hills, much less mountains. I've always lacked the ability, if not willingness, to pedal any faster than six M.P.H. The *ciclismo* (chee-KLEES-moh) club members often average 15 M.P.H. riding down *and* up mountains. Rich joined the UIC (Unione Internazionale Cicloscalatori) – an international cycling group – and is the first person from the U.S. to do so. I am thankful Rich found a cycling group in general, and Giordano in particular, who challenges his skills and abilities. Rich is not only a good cyclist for a guy pushing sixty, but also can give cyclists half his age a run for the summit. Because of that chance meeting in the tourist information center, Rich is happy and I am even happier.

The cycling club also gets together for social outings which Giordano insists I attend. One evening I find myself sitting at a long table in a pizza parlor surrounded by twenty-five male cyclists between the ages of thirty and eighty, and one female cyclist. Not one other spouse shows. Still, I enjoy myself, watching the good-natured, though over-my-head, banter. Whenever I say anything in Italian, my seatmates act like I'd just biked up a mountain. They rave and laugh every time I open my mouth. The experience empowers me. Now I yak in Italian whenever I get the chance. Of course, this leads me into many misunderstandings but, thankfully, next to food, Italians love a good laugh.

Another cycling social event begins at six o'clock with a city council meeting. Cycling club members and city elders gather on the second floor of an ancient building that used to hold prisoners in its dungeon. Its rooms upstairs now house offices and meeting rooms. After more than an hour of socializing before the meeting even starts, everyone finally settles into their seats. Right before the official business gets underway, a team of teenage cyclists walks in dressed in red cycling gear. They sit in a place of honor in the front row of the audience. The city solons and cycling elders tout an upcoming cycling event they are giving expressly for the city's youth (ages 10-19). The room we sit in, with its high ceiling, beautifully carved moldings and art hanging on its walls, keeps me occupied through the lengthy speeches.

Afterward, everyone leaves and reconvenes at a local restaurant where I'm surprised to see that several hundred more people – parents and their children, even babies (future cyclists of Italy) – have already gathered. It's a school night and it looks as though we've entered a wedding reception.

Three large banquet rooms, set up with long tables, are already filled with people. Dinner starts around eight o'clock. By the time dessert is served, around eleven, the children are red-faced from running all over the place. Three toddlers happily sit in a dry display fountain tossing rocks around. I can't imagine any of the student cyclists getting up the next day in time for school.

Clemenza.

By the end of the year, Clemenza and Giordano will have accompanied us to classical music events, invited us for dinner and asked us to join an informal walking group that treks up to a nearby spa, *Terme di Fontecchio*, for coffee each morning.

A much-needed break from the mind-breaking language immersion comes from Luigi and Nadia, owners of *Trattoria Il Feudo,* who both speak English. We met them because of one act of generosity that snowballed until our calendar ran over with friends.

Soon after we arrived in January, Giuseppe asked if we'd like to borrow his and his wife's bikes stored in the basement of the old mansion where we had lived the first two months. These bikes are not to be confused with the lightweight road bikes members of the cycling club ride. These sturdy two-wheelers are built for tooling around town, running errands or taking leisurely rides on the dirt path next to the river. Having planned to purchase two secondhand utilitarian bikes ourselves, Giuseppe's offer was a bountiful surprise.

With key in hand, Giuseppe led us down steep stone stairs to the basement of the mansion. This was no ordinary cellar, but more like catacombs, half of which was located below street level and half at street level. Webs of dirt hung from the ceiling like stalactites. One hundred years ago, these two-foot-thick walls, whitewashed with plaster, housed farm animals, evidenced by two barn doors. Between the barn doors and the cement footing of the basement floor there is enough space for cats to get through, but no sign, or smell, of any, and no telltale signs of mice or rats either.

Giuseppe opened one of the barn doors to allow light in, and then returned into the darkness and unlocked a padlocked door. When the bikes came into view my heart leaped – they were just like the old dusty one featured in the movie *Il Postino* (The Postman). Junkers from the past, one speed with hand brakes, and mine had a basket on the front. How very Sophia! I envisioned myself riding home from the fruit-and-vegetable market with a bouquet of flowers lying across the top, the sun on my head, and the vision even had me in a skirt!

Left alone with our "new" bikes, Rich tinkered with them, noting they were in pretty good shape except for one tire on the woman's bike; it was flat due to a broken valve.

The following cold, damp Saturday, late in the afternoon when businesses usually reopened, we walked the bike to the repair shop inside the ancient city, bumping it over cobblestones along the way. The bike shop always had its "open" sign hanging in the window, yet for all the times we'd walked past it, we had yet to see it open. This day was no different.

As we stood outside under a gray sky, the empty street seemed foreboding compared to its usual morning busyness. We wondered if the owner might still be on Italy's extended lunch hour. Saturday seemed like a perfect day to be open for customers who worked all week. After ten minutes of waiting, I noticed a light on in the restaurant across the narrow street. While I stood guard over my treasured bicycle – I probably could've left it there all night and no one would've taken it – Rich entered the restaurant.

Trying to be helpful, I called after him. "Ask them, *'Quando il negozio delle biciclette apre?'*"

Less than a minute later, he emerged, accompanied by a slightly balding, roundish Italian man in his late he found out so quickly that the guy spoke English. Apparently, he had ignored my prompt to speak Italian and, instead, entered the restaurant asking, "Do you speak English?") Despite the chill in the air, the restaurant owner stood cross-armed on the stoop, leaving the door wide open.

He talked nonstop, telling us first about the bike shop owner, then how he'd lived and worked as a chef in Canada for fifteen years, and now in Città di Castello for almost four. Soon his wife Nadia joined us and we introduced ourselves. Nadia, though born in Canada, looks as Italian as her husband, with her dark chocolate eyes, a cook's bonnet taming her long black hair, and a bib apron tied around her waist. Along with her native English, she also speaks fluent Italian since her parents hail from Venice. She and I would come to exchange books in English – a source of great joy to me.

Soon after 9/11, when the couple still lived and worked in Canada, they agreed to leave the rat race, be their own boss and open a high-end restaurant in Umbria.

Nadia & Luigi.

Luigi tells us of the many important people who have eaten in his restaurant, the most notable diner being Lance Armstrong. He speaks of his culinary art with deep passion, and we learn his mother, Grazia, who is technically retired, helps out once in awhile. They give us their phone number and tell us to call them any time we need assistance.

Already the gift of the bicycles spawned one pair of angels who speak both English and Italian – along with books, in English. But the gifts didn't stop there.

We return later that evening (sans bicycle) for what will be our first of many delightful dinners at *Il Feudo*. After dinner, Luigi and Nadia kiss our cheeks while saying goodbye at the front door of the restaurant – Italians make fast friends. As I turn, something catches our eye across the street at the bike shop. The area is lit up like a carnival. Not only are the bike shop's lights on, but it is open. It is 10 p.m. on a Saturday night and it is open! Too mellowed from the food and wine to walk briskly, we amble over and make an appointment to bring the lame bike back for a valve job the following Monday.

If all this isn't enough serendipity, Luigi and Nadia would later introduce us to two semi-retired Floridians, Peter and Marsha. For a few months every year, they live in the house they had restored, two medieval

Marsha and Peter with Teri, a seller of olive oils in Trevi.

blocks from *Il Feudo*. Their place on the second floor is not only across from an active bocce ball court, but also has a terrace and large garden where they dine while watching the goings-on of their vibrant neighborhood. They often invite us to dinner and their generosity toward everyone seems endless.

Later, Peter joins Rich and Giordano for strenuous bike rides in the mountains, and when Peter and Marsha's son and daughter-in-law come for a visit, they too follow Giordano as though he were the Pied Piper. Marsha and I stay behind; she happily puttering in her garden and I happily reading. Marsha has come to own an impressive library due to the books she brings with her from Florida coupled with those left behind by visitors. Thanks to Peter and Marsha having a car, all four of us enjoy cultural events and explore nearby towns together.

At first, Peter, Marsha, Rich and I were so determined to assimilate into the culture that we greeted each other with the customary two-cheeked kiss. American custom has it that on your approach to hug someone you move to your left (toward their right shoulder) and they do likewise, which makes for a clean embrace. In Italy, the two-cheeked kiss begins by moving to your right (toward the person's left shoulder and supposedly closer to their heart) so you can press your left cheek (or lips) to his or her left cheek. Then both people switch to press right cheek (or lips) to right cheek. This is totally opposite to what Americans have been conditioned to do. After a misstep

Sandro Galvani.

Tullio Pavanelli and Sandro Belletti.

on either Peter's or Rich's part (no one will take responsibility) which ended with a slight brushing of lips, the two laughingly agreed to greet each other like Americans – with a handshake.

Acquiring so many upbeat and delightful friends so early in our stay adds a charm to the place one can't get by just visiting. It boggles my mind to think how many people came into our lives without me once putting "Make Friends" on my to-do list. My A-type personality is beginning to cozy up to this Italian *Che serà, serà!* lifestyle. Every time I recall the chain of events, spawned by Giuseppe's generosity in lending us two old bikes, one of which thankfully needed repair, followed by one closed repair shop, I'm filled with gratitude. ❤

13

GETTING TO TOWN

Even when Rich is with me, I feel conspicuous waiting at the bus stop – a three-minute walk down a dirt road from Macrì. It's not like I've never waited for a bus before; I waited for plenty in Chicago where I grew up. The difference is that in Chicago a person stands on a sidewalk to catch a bus. The bus stop near our country apartment requires us to stand on a grate that spans a drainage ditch. The grate is a half-foot higher than the two-lane highway bisecting a patchwork of farm fields, and though I am thankful we don't have to stand on the roadway itself, I feel funny up here watching the people in their cars staring at us as they speed by.

Whenever the traffic dies down while we're waiting, the serenity of the valley takes our breath away. We stand between a set of mountain ranges just the right distance away to be impressive while, at the same time, making the sky look much grander than we urban dwellers are accustomed to.

The grate, and therefore the bus stop, is on the opposite side of the road from where the bus will be coming around a curve. Waiting on the grate on the wrong side of the road allows the bus driver to see us in time to stop without having to slam on his brakes. While the bus rolls to a halt, I scurry and Rich lopes across the street in front of it and we climb aboard.

If I am with Rich while boarding the bus, the driver keeps his eyes straight ahead and grumbles, *"Buon giorno."* If I board alone, the driver looks at me and smiles as he cheerfully says, *"Buon giorno!"*

For the most part we take the bus to and from town; otherwise we walk the three miles along the two-lane highway. Either way, this is not what I'd envisioned before coming to Italy. Ever since I'd watched the movie *Il Postino* in 1995, before our first trip overseas, my vision always saw me walking – or riding a bike – to town on a quiet country road. I did not once imagine walking alongside the same road buses, cars and 18-wheelers take to town. This highway doesn't even have a shoulder to walk on. Instead, a narrow strip of dusty, or muddy – depending on the weather – grass falls off into a steep, weedy ditch. Sunglasses are required, even on cloudy days, or dirt from the road flies in my eyes. Each time a truck is about to pass, I fear the force of its draft might suck my body onto its side panel and carry me into town like Garfield plastered to a car window.

There is, however, a peaceful, tree-lined footpath alongside the Tiber River. We had walked short sections of it now and again when we lived in Giuseppe's apartment. The nice thing about living there was that the town was, as one would expect, on the same side of the river as the footpath. The problem with living in the country is that although we can see the swath of cleared forest the river makes, the path is on the other side of the river.

There are two car bridges in the vicinity that cross the river, but they are equidistant from where we live. The bridge closest to town requires two miles of walking on the highway before having to hop a guardrail and navigate down a steep embankment onto the path to continue the last mile to town.

Me standing on the grate, waiting for the bus to come from the opposite direction. The building in the distance, right behind the bus stop post, is Macrì Country House.

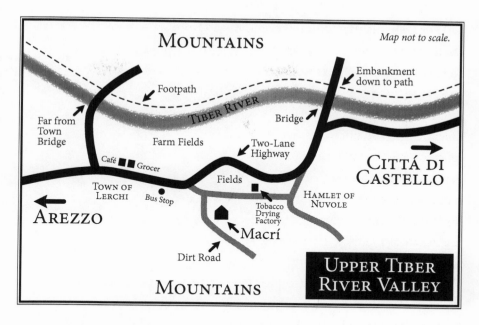

The second bridge is two miles from Macrì in the opposite direction from town, but requires only one mile of walking on the busy highway before turning onto a less-traveled one. This route will deliver us to the path without having to make our way down an embankment. I like the idea of going this way even if it is longer.

I obsess about finding a footpath that keeps me from having to step on what I've come to consider the "evil highway." Finding a better way becomes my purpose in life. My obsessing is probably why Rich goes along with my idea to try walking to the faraway bridge and then taking the path all the way into town. Although it will take longer, it could be pleasant. After all, we are retired now. All we have is time. We estimate it will take an hour-and-a-half, tops.

We set out walking to the small village of Lerchi a hundred yards past the bus stop, away from Città di Castello. A few hundred people live here and it has a church whose bells we are fortunate enough to hear from our apartment.

Once we pass the little grocery store, church and cemetery, we come to farm fields. Next we pass one of those large three-story stone houses that are often pictured on calendars and postcards. The setting would be idyllic except for it being situated a few yards from the road. We have to remind ourselves that three hundred years ago, this highway was merely a dirt path the width of a carriage.

The church in nearby Lerchi.

In the distance we see another stone house set even closer to the highway. As we approach, a large German shepherd barks wildly at us from his narrow dog run beside the house. Our sightline is then drawn up to the dog's owners, a man and woman, who are leaning on a windowsill watching us advance as though they've been expecting us.

As we approach, the woman waves and yells a hearty British, "Hallo!" over the sound of traffic. Upon our reaching them, she gently elbows the man and says, "I told you they weren't Italian." The next thing we know we are sitting in their kitchen sipping tea. Dawn works at the school *Lingua Più* where we take Italian lessons (she's fluent in Italian and teaches English there), and her husband, Lorenzo, a construction worker, is the first native Roman I've ever met. They've been married twenty-two years, have three children (two "at university" as the Brits are wont to say), and Lorenzo is home recuperating from back surgery. They rent their living quarters; the entire second floor of the old stone house. Another family lives above them. On the ground floor, are storage areas and separate stairways to each flat.

Dawn and Lorenzo give us a tour of the house, ending any romantic ideas I had had about these dwellings. Black fungus dots every interior white wall, and it isn't the kind of fungi one eats and pays dearly for in Italian restaurants.

Pointing to a wall in their bedroom, Dawn says, "It almost looks like a map of the world, wouldn't you say?" She rushes over to point out Italy and England and we nod our heads. It does look like a map or maybe a collection of Rorschach tests.

We were walking between a truck like this and the stone wall when we saw Dawn and Lorenzo leaning out of the second floor window.

In addition, they add, it costs a fortune to heat their one floor. They confess they go to bed wearing both a sweater and a coat. I understand. I've been wearing a sweat suit to bed and only feel warm because of it and the fact that Rich throws off heat like a furnace. We've also experienced the horrific expense of paying 400 euros (nearly 500 U.S. dollars) for three weeks of heating our three-room apartment at 68 degrees. After that shock, we dialed down to 59 during the day, and turn it totally off at night. (Okay, I push it up now and again, but only for a few minutes, just to heat up the radiators. There's only so much wine a person can drink to stay warm.)

The thing about stone walls is that they retain the outdoor temperature for long periods of time. Since our country apartment hadn't been occupied all winter, and we moved into it in mid-March, it took weeks of heating the place to rid the walls of the damp. Likewise in summer, once the walls heat up, it takes longer for them to cool down. That's one reason Italians keep their shutters closed all day in summer when the sun is out – to shut out at least some of the heat. Shutters also act like screens, keeping bugs from flying in. Italians don't seem to mind living with their windows open (the better to keep the fungus away) and no heat in the winter and living in dark houses during the summer. They, along with Rich, are much more tolerant of large temperature swings than I am.

After an enjoyable conversation with Dawn and Lorenzo, we continue our journey toward the bridge, hoping to be delivered to the peaceful path on the other side of the Tiber River. By now, we have turned onto a much quieter two-lane highway. Looking back at the old stone house, I hope with all my heart that the many recently restored stone houses we see scattered about the countryside don't cost as much to heat and don't have that awful black "wall art" going on.

This is how retirement is. You run into something interesting and suddenly the plans you made that morning vaporize and you don't care one whit if they change completely. Such luxury to stop for an unplanned tea break.

Once we cross a bridge that brings us over what appears to be the Tiber River, I insist the next dirt road is the trailhead and Rich, being the sweet guy he is, follows me onto it. Fifteen minutes later, we find ourselves in the middle of a farmer's field and at a dead-end. What we'd crossed turned out to be a tributary of the river. We backtrack and continue walking and Rich, sweet guy that he is, doesn't utter a peep although I know he knew I'd been mistaken the moment I insisted on taking that dead-end path.

After another long stretch of highway, we cross another bridge and come to the sign announcing the correct path. At long last we start heading toward town. This public path alongside the river is similar to the ones constructed in the U.S. by the Rails-to-Trails Conservancy, only the conservancy's paths follow old train beds instead of rivers.

A variety of substances make up the path's surface: gravel, crushed stone, dirt, grass, packed mud and wet muddy mud, depending on recent rains and snow melt from the mountains. On our right the river flows; sometimes mirror smooth, sometimes churning rapids. On our left are farm fields, stands of trees, an occasional house and, always, in the distance, the mountains, one still snow covered in April.

Someone with a good arm could throw a stone across the river, that's how narrow it is. This makes me ask myself (and anyone who will listen): "Would it be so hard to build a footbridge and save us from having to walk the evil highway?"

More than three-and-a-half hours from the time we leave our apartment, we enter the walls of Città di Castello. Three-and-a half hours! Even accounting for the wrong turn and the visit with Dawn and Lorenzo, it seems incredibly long until we calculate that we've walked more than seven miles. ♥

14

BIKING TO TOWN

It's a Sunday in April and we need to go into town to make our weekly phone calls home. We start out in the morning on our borrowed bikes. We think that instead of walking, the bikes might be faster, giving us a better chance of returning in daylight.

We pedal the narrow two-lane highway for a couple of miles toward town, then cross the bridge over the Tiber River. We dismount and Rich carries our bikes, one at a time, down the steep embankment to the pretty path that follows the river into town.

We could have continued on the highway, but even without buses or trucks running on Sundays, it remains dangerously narrow. Besides, the path's beauty never fails to enchant us.

Surprised to see that kayak races are being held on the river, we stop awhile and watch. As we draw closer to town, more and more spectators impede our progress.

In town we are again surprised when we arrive in the main piazza where a humungous antique fair is

The Tiber River.

going on. We eat our mid-day Sunday meal at a nice restaurant, *Il Preludio*, and hurriedly return to Piazza Matteotti to peruse the bazaar offerings. The variety of heavy wooden armoires and dazzling candelabras, chandeliers, and fireplace utensils draws us in. Everywhere we turn, tables laden with antique brass, crystal, and wood beckon to be admired. Before we know it, four o'clock rolls around and we still haven't started our phone calls.

At the Internet Point, other callers fill all ten phone booths. Usually Rich takes one booth and I another so we can do two calls at once. The wait, coupled with our newly adopted *che serà serà* state of mind, allows the sun to set while we blissfully fill up on news from home.

When we step out of the Internet Point, I say, "Holy cow! Look how dark it's getting. Where has the day gone." It feels as though we left Macrì only a few hours ago.

We decide to ride the highway all the way home, instead of taking the longer way on the riverside path. Outside of town where there are no street lamps, I notice that the light on my bike isn't half as bright as I'd like it to be. Besides, whenever I stop pedaling it dims to nothingness. Because Rich's bike has neither a light nor a reflector and my bike has both, I bring up the rear. We hope at least a little light will be cast in front of Rich so he can stay on the roadway.

Despite pedaling at an easy pace on level ground my heart pounds with anxiety. I follow the shred of white I can see emanating from Rich's shirt as he pedals in front of me. Blessedly, an oncoming car comes toward us, lighting both its lane and ours. After it passes, another one comes from behind and it, too, illuminates the path, but I worry it won't see us. It safely passes.

At the next curve, I see the light of an oncoming car and the light from one approaching behind us. I worry they will meet exactly where we are, and they do. They whiz past each other and us at fifty miles per hour. Their draft stirs up dirt and blows my hair. After their lights fade, I can no longer see Rich. Has he pulled ahead of me or has it gotten darker? The only light is the sickly one emanating from my bike. Beyond it is pure blackness. I can barely see beyond my front tire. After a minute or two of riding blind, I feel the road rising under me and I need to pedal harder. I pray I don't ride into a ditch and I pray my heart and lungs have the strength to power me home.

I still can't see Rich and the rise now feels like a hill. I stand and press the pedals with all my might but still the bicycle slows. Even with all my weight placed on alternating pedals, the bike rolls to a stop. Panting, I walk it to the side of the road. Still straddling the bike, I fold my body

Rich on the borrowed bike from Giuseppe.

over the guardrail, gasping for breath, gasping with fear. I look up, and at the top of the hill, which is really only a rise, I see Rich's silhouette against the western sky. Although he has stopped to wait for me, I feel rage. I don't understand where it's coming from. He always waits for me. He never berates me for being slow. Not once in thirty-two years and hundreds of hikes and bike trails has he ever said, "Hurry up."

Then it comes to me. I am jealous. I am jealous of his physical strength and I am jealous of his quiet strength and I am jealous of his patience with me. I have none of these qualities and I covet them. It is, as the Buddha says, desire that creates all pain and suffering. And I desire what Rich has and I know it will take me lifetimes to achieve the quiet strength and patience he embodies. How long will it take me to accept that I'll never ever have his physical strength?

I walk my bike up the rest of the hill – a hill that didn't even resemble a hill when we rode down it from the other direction this morning. I have no memory of coasting.

When I reach Rich, he silently climbs back onto his bike and continues.

As I've done a hundred times before, I follow him. I know the lump in my throat comes from my stubbornness – I don't ever want to be vulnerable. My heart hurts, not from pedaling so hard, but from the space Rich allows me to own my fears. ♥

15

FINDING MY WAY

Despite that scary ride home in the dark, the river and footpath still beckon me. The following Monday, when I finish running errands in town, I decide that instead of walking the highway home, I'll take the pretty path next to the river as far as the bridge. I go by myself since Rich wants to work out at the gym first.

After a delightful stretch of trees arcing over the path, the river running alongside it, I come to the car bridge closest to Macrì. I veer off the path onto a tractor trail and claw my way up the steep, slippery embankment next to the bridge. I need to grab small trees and tufts of grass for support. At the top, I wipe off my muddy shoes as best as I can in the overgrown grass and, with as much aplomb as I can muster, swing one leg over the guardrail and then the other, as cars speed by. I walk across the wide bridge (and thus over the river) and along the two-lane highway. Macrì is still two miles away.

It is during this stretch when the honking starts.

I haven't been honked at since I was in my twenties. For one mad moment I think it might be because my backside could be pleasing to the Italian truck drivers whipping around the narrow two-lane highway I'm trekking. Before I can even savor this possibility, approaching trucks start honking too. In my heart I know truck drivers don't honk at 57-year-old women whose faces are visible. I dare to look up at the next driver barreling toward me. I see him drumming his forefinger to his temple as if to say,

Me, on another day, walking down the embankment.

"Pazza" (Crazy!) Never mind that every time I see a semi coming I step off the highway into the grass and stop walking. Never mind that Rich can walk the very same highway, never move an inch off the white line painted on the border of the pavement, and not get honked at once.

Again the resentment rises in my throat. Why are men always given more leeway than women? "See," I say out loud to myself, "even in paradise your problems find you." You can change locale, even change your name, but no matter how much you pretend everything is fresh and new, unless you deal with the feelings of your past, the resentment will live on and on.

Upon reflection, I think it is probably a collective resentment. I remember the time Rich and I had to stand through a parents' meeting in the school gym. My cramps were so bad I had to lean heavily against the wall, fighting to keep from passing out and slumping to the floor. Meanwhile, I looked at Rich in front of me, standing without assistance, standing without effort or pain. Fairly or not, for all women who came before me, and all women living now, and all women who have yet to be born, I resented him and *all* men for that difference. Not only did I feel resentment at that moment, I now acknowledge having had that feeling on and off throughout my life.

Another truck whips by. As I continue to walk, it occurs to me that I'm not only endangering my life, but the truckers' and other drivers' lives as well. My muscles, already knotted, tighten up more. If two 18-wheelers are traveling toward each other, and I am standing at the same place in the road where their paths cross, there'd be no wiggle room if, say, a gust of wind pulled one of them off course. I conclude that my presence scares the poor truck drivers as much as it scares me.

I scurry around one bend and then another. All I wish is to get off this highway. This is precisely when my wish comes true, only it doesn't come in the form I expect. I see Quinto and Liana's car pass me on their way, no doubt, to their country house. Quinto brakes hard and pulls to the side of the road as best he can. The back end of his car sticks out enough to keep a truck from passing. In a matter of seconds, traffic backs up. I run to reach the car's passenger side. Liana's face, framed in the open window, registers fear … for my safety. I hop into the back seat where "Deke" eagerly greets me, and as I slam the door, the car takes off, its wheels throwing debris out from behind it. Quinto drives me the rest of the way to Macrì, all the while lecturing me about the dangers of walking the highway. I don't understand a word of his Italian, but I know exactly what his stern words are saying. Stubbornly, in my defense I tell them how much I like to walk, as though that's a good excuse. I feel like their child.

This only serves to bring up another one of my issues. Quinto's dress-down reminds me of how my father used to yell at me. I squeeze my eyes shut, grit my teeth. If I admit he is right, my pride will be hurt, and that recognition of pride always leads to the most painful of feelings … shame.

By the time I put the key in the door of our apartment, my nerves are jangling like nobody's business.

Upstairs, I throw the key down on the table and plop into a chair. I give up. Why don't I face it? There is no quiet road that leads from our apartment to town. I hate giving up.

There's truth in the adage, "Sleep on it." The next morning, I recall Rich saying that he had jogged a little dirt road that runs directly in front of Macrì. I'm pleased that although I've given up, my subconscious hasn't. I ask him about the road. He says it doesn't go far and ends near the tobacco-drying factory. At that point it changes from pavement to dirt and looks as though it is private.

I have no reason to go into town, so Rich goes by himself. Instead I walk in the opposite direction to the little grocery store in Lerchi. I'm desperate for Perugian chocolates and can't believe I'd let myself run out. On my return, I bypass the turn-in to Macrì and continue walking on the pavement where Rich had jogged. Even if the road turns into a dead end, I think it is charming enough to be used for little walks, perhaps for after-dinner strolls when it gets warmer, should it ever get warmer.

Once I reach the part of the road that looks decidedly private – a deeply rutted, narrow farm road – I stop. I see the tobacco-drying factory on my left, surrounded by a wrought-iron fence and tall pine trees. Except for two yappy dogs, it stands deserted. Should I continue walking even if it means trespassing? What if the dogs can get out of an opening I can't see?

The farm road wends its way down to a creek which needs to be rock-stepped across.

The bridge is just around the curve.

The crowded two-lane highway.

The road coming down from the farm road and Nuvole.

Would they attack? They don't sound friendly at all.

I stand there, considering what to do when I hear a car rumbling behind me. My heart does a double beat, my mind envisioning an angry person yelling at me for trespassing. It occurs to me that I'm always worried people are going to yell at me. Conditioned by my childhood, and reinforced by Quinto, I immediately devise my defense for trespassing – *Sto solo guardando. Abito là, a Macrì* (I'm only looking. I live over there, at Macrì). I step off the road into the weeds and turn to watch an old green Citröen slowly rumble past. I duck to look inside and see an old woman twist her head around to stare at me, her mouth a straight line. The car slows to a crawl, and I think, *Now I'm really in for it.* Then, from somewhere deep inside me, courage rises and I hustle around to her side of the car. She comes to a full stop and rolls down her window. I greet her with a polite

"*Buon giorno, Signora,*" and ask if the road we are on is private. "*È questa strada privata?*" Her face spreads into the loveliest smile. Why no, the road is not private. But, she adds, it doesn't go all the way into town, if that's what I planned to do. What, I wonder, would make her think that? I tell her I'm just out for a walk and she nods, saying, "*Buona passeggiata,*" (Have a good walk) and drives away. I watch the hips of the car jostle over the ruts.

My nerves are calmer now. I follow where the car has gone, on the dusty road that threads between peaceful farm fields. The wind gales through this part of the valley, and the sky domes over me, placing me in the middle of nature's drama. For a long time I stand still, feeling the clean wind whisk over my face and through my hair. I admire the bluish mountains in the distance and … and … heaven of mercy! I spot the two-lane evil highway off to my left, running parallel to the road I'm standing on. This is a good sign, but I continue to hold my breath, not daring to hope this farm road goes far enough to be of any use. Slowly, I continue to follow it. It curves and dips down into a shady forested area where there is a pounding waterfall and a creek flowing over the road. The creek is shallow enough for me to rock-step across. One hundred yards later, negotiating deep but dry ruts, I continue moving forward while keeping my eye on the highway.

At last, I emerge at the top of a hill where a paved road slopes down. Bending my knees slightly, I walk downhill (a sign says it is a ten percent grade) past several houses, all with barking dogs behind fences. At the bottom of the hill is the evil highway. But, what's exciting is that from here I can see the car bridge that crosses the river to the embankment that leads down to the footpath. The old woman in the Citröen was right; the road doesn't go all the way into town but the bridge that connects to the path is not more than a quarter mile from where I stand! I look at the sign next to me, announcing the tiny hamlet as *Nuvole* (clouds). I'd seen that sign before, while walking past it and while on the bus, but had never paid much attention to the road and houses beyond it. I look again to double check how close the car bridge is from where I stand. Tears of relief and joy fill my eyes. Walking one hundred yards alongside a busy highway isn't nearly as bad as walking miles on it.

I return home the same way I came, tears streaming down my cheeks, thinking how fortuitous it was that the old woman drove by when I so needed an angel for reassurance, and how all along, the little voice inside me knew there was an answer to my prayers. ♥

16

THE BRIDGE RETURNS...
IN A DIFFERENT FORM

One evening, while entertaining Marsha and Peter outdoors of our apartment at Macrì, one of my dental bridges falls out. Thankfully, there's no pain. I tuck the bridge into my napkin.

I don't take events like these lightly. I believe scientists will some day prove that our maladies often relate to how we're thinking. As it happens, my thinking has felt unsettled lately.

The morning after my bridge falls out, I sit at my computer, positioned under our open bedroom window. I can't bring myself to do anything but stare outside. A large pot of purple petunias, bought in town and carried home on the bus, fills the window sill. When I gaze over their velvet heads trembling in the wind, I see a hill carpeted with varying shades of green grasses, red poppies, yellow buttercups and Queen Anne's lace. Beyond the hill, a dense forest of trees tops a mountain in a ragged eyebrow. Blue sky fills the top third of the window. A tender breeze, warmed by the springtime sun, floats in, envelops me in a fresh coat of air.

To be sad on a cold rainy day is one thing. To be sad on a day like this is tragic.

My husband is upset with me ... and I with him, and I don't know how to put things right.

The difficulty in our marriage repeats itself like a wallpaper pattern. It starts with me commenting on something Rich has done – something as innocuous as forgetting something at the store. See, I make a list so I won't forget. My thinking is: Why doesn't he see that *my* way is better? My tone implies, "Holy mackerel, I can't believe how stupid you are!" I don't mean to say it that way but it comes out that way. It's a conditioned response. It's a knee-jerk reaction. It's a terrible habit. Since I don't intentionally set out to hurt him, I wonder what unconscious part of me manages to consistently do so.

As a youngster, I remember people saying how clever and funny I was. My repartee, sharpened and refined by living with two adults – my mother and father – and a brother six years older than I, came to define me. In a word, our family dynamic could be defined as "snarky." Sarcasm became my defense. I'm not complaining, I'm just explaining.

Soon after we married, Rich pointed out how hurtful sarcasm is. For more than three decades, I pooh-poohed his observation, which he repeated sporadically. From my perspective, he had no sense of humor. As a result, every time I made a remark that pegged him as "stupid" – considered the worst thing one could say to another person in the family I grew up in – he withdrew. I wanted to argue with him like my parents had argued with each other and with my brother and me, but he wouldn't participate. This, of course, only made me angrier.

Each time he stonewalled me I decided I could just as easily stonewall him. After all, when my mother gave me the silent treatment, she could not have hurt me more.

Disagreement or no disagreement, bridge or no bridge, Rich and I ready ourselves to hop the bus to town for our Italian class. We don't discuss whether or not to go. This where we're alike – you've committed to something and you see it through. Our exchanges, however, have devolved to the bare minimum. When we do speak, we do so in what I call "polite speak." It's kind but it's phony at the same time.

Sitting next to the window on the bus, watching the farm fields and wild flowers whir by, I think how uncomfortable this polite talk is, how it knots my chest. I've come far enough to know he's right – that sarcastic remarks are hurtful. But I can't seem to stop myself. The moment the words leave my mouth I know what I've done. I want to reach out and reel them in. Since coming to Italy, where either my senses have grown sharper or Rich has become less subtle, I now perceive a tensing of his body, a slight leaning away from me, whenever I say things that have even a hint of blame in them. Like never before, I see the hurt in his eyes and, at the same time, my regret – and, of course, shame – grows exponentially to his hurt.

At class, our teacher, Roberta, kindly recommends her dentist and makes an appointment for me. His office is next door to the language school.

That afternoon, with my bridge safely tucked in a Baggie and clutched in my fist, I go alone to see the kindly dentist. I'm practical that way. No sense both of us losing a beautiful day.

In less than five minutes the dentist pantomimes, and I guess, what the problem is. We'd make a great team playing Charades.

The post, onto which the bridge had been anchored, broke. Underneath, only a slip of a tooth remains. The bridge itself is still intact but a new post needs to be implanted.

As the dentist continues to pantomime and speak, I keep hearing the Italian word *ospedale* (hospital). I can't imagine how the hospital could be involved in this.

As he continues to talk, the fog surrounding his words lifts. He is trying to explain that I must go to the hospital with his prescription to get my mouth X-rayed. We are both relieved when I finally understand.

Before leaving, he glues the bridge back into place, tells me to be careful (no hard-crusted *bruschetta* for awhile) and we'll reconvene for another game of Charades once I return with the X-ray in hand.

I ask him how much I owe him and he says, *"Niente."* Nothing.

Feeling pretty perky with my bridge back in, I decide to walk to the hospital. I don't know where it is, but I've seen road signs all over town for it. Besides, I'm footloose and fancy free ... well, except for the heartache.

While walking I think how being in Italy, where few people speak

English, where Rich and I have fewer responsibilities and interruptions, and where we're with each other so many more hours than usual, our accumulated scars from the past rub a hurtful spur that can no longer be ignored. While the muscle of our team unit (our common philosophies and backgrounds) stays strong and firm, the skeleton on which we hang things is showing signs of fracture.

More than an hour, and many kilometers, later under a white-hot sun, I see the hospital, built on a hill in the hinterlands, surrounded by farm houses and fields. As I approach, I see five horses, their coats shining under the sun, peacefully munching hay in a fenced-in field. As I cross the parking lot, I hear a rooster crow. It sounds out of place, it being nearly two o'clock in the afternoon, and only minutes by car from town. Despite being overheated, I have to chuckle. I'm a city girl. I thought roosters only crowed at dawn.

The hospital near Città di Castello.

I show the prescription to the woman at the information desk and she gives me directions. Easy to find. In another area on the main floor, I stand outside a room and take a number, as though I'm in a bakery, and wait less than five minutes to be waited on.

When I hand the prescription to the clerk, I learn that I need to make an appointment for the X-ray to be taken on a future day. I should have known it wouldn't be easy. Once she and I agree on an appointment date and time, another problem arises. No, it isn't insurance or lack of it, or the fact I am foreign or that the young woman behind the desk can barely understand me or I her. No, the problem is that I don't have a family doctor in Italy. Before I can have the X-ray, she insists I must procure a family doctor.

Instead of using words, I plead my case emotionally. I allow my expression to border on breaking down, which is easy given the hot, seemingly endless walk I'd just completed, sweat dripping unbecomingly from my scalp and face. She picks up the phone. Five minutes of nerve-jangling chatter later, a higher-up assures her that a family doctor isn't a requirement to X-ray a tooth. She jots down the appointment time for the next day, hands it to me, and I hoof my way back to town. Things are looking up … again.

Rich and I are still only speaking politely. Since I have to return to the hospital to have the X-ray taken, he helps me figure out which local bus to take. The thermometer is tripping ninety. No need to walk again.

❧

The following day, I pass through no fewer than twenty doors to check in for the X-ray. Not one door is automatic, not even the first one leading in from outdoors. After I check in, the woman behind the counter gives me directions where to go and wait. All I hear is *"Sala Quattro"* (Room 4) and *"Sala Cinque"* (Room 5) and, *"Al fondo del corridoio e giri a destra."* (At the end of the corridor, make a right.) Turning the corner at the end of the hall, I notice a row of dressing room doors lining the wall on my right. Room 4 is occupied, as flagged by the red indicator on the doorknob. I enter Room 5 and lock the door behind me. Another door, on the opposite wall, has been left ajar and I can see it leads to an X-ray room. Certain I don't have to take my clothes off, I pull a book from my backpack, hang the backpack on a hook, and sit in the folding chair and read.

Soon a chunky woman with a clipboard in her hand pokes her head in and, in a deep voice, demands to know who I am. When I tell her my name, she glances at her clipboard and up at me again, asking what is to be X-rayed. I point inside my mouth. Not so gently she takes me by the elbow, unlocks the door and, as she steers me, I reach behind and grab my backpack off the hook. In the corridor, she sternly points to the bank of chairs opposite the changing rooms. I had been so focused on finding *Sala*

Quattro and *Sala Cinque* that I hadn't noticed the chairs before. A teenage boy rises and takes my place in Room 5. Embarrassed, I sit on the edge of the seat, back straight, clutching my backpack.

Within a few minutes, a young man, who tells me his name is Mateo, emerges from yet another door and leads me into a room reminiscent of a basement with its concrete floor and lack of ceiling tiles to cover the infrastructure of the building. Gently, he unclasps my necklace and carefully hands it to me. I am surprised to be led to a gargantuan X-ray machine. I remain standing, pressing my chin and forehead against the appropriate rests as instructed. Mateo tells me to hold still and leaves to the safety of his control room. To my amazement, the machine makes a 360-degree trip around my head. Mateo quickly returns and says to come back tomorrow to pick up the X-ray. Oh, great. Another trip to the hospital.

Once again I need to stand in the "bakery" line, take a number and wait my turn. The X-ray needs to be paid for here before it can be picked up. The good news, though, is that it only costs five euros!

After three trips to the hospital, I return to see il Dottore Pierone to play another game of Charades. The root of the tooth with the broken post is infected and the dentist recommends extraction, followed by a standard waiting period of three months for things to settle down before the placing of an implant and a crown.

Back in town, at the Internet Point where there's a bank of phones, I call my dentist at home and make an appointment for a telephone consult. When we talk, he explains my options. Together we decide to get the infected tooth extracted as soon as possible and, since there is a long wait before the next procedure can be done, I'll wait to have the rest done when I return to the U.S.

A few days later, while Rich sits in the waiting room, the dentist injects Novacain, waits several minutes, then calmly hammers the tooth until it cracks open like a walnut. He extracts one piece after another, making sure to show me the infected root clinging to the end of one piece. Thankfully, these things do not bother me.

The appointment began around 6:30 p.m. (the dentist's hours are 2:30 to 9:30 p.m.), after the local buses stop running. Earlier in the day, Rich had arranged with our town's one-and-only taxi driver to bring us home from the dentist. Rich didn't want me walking three miles after the procedure. Disagreement or no disagreement, he is always kind.

With the procedure painlessly finished, Dr. Pierone gives me an ice pack to press against my cheek. He calls the cab, which makes life a lot easier for everyone because he can explain to the cabbie where the office is located. We want to pay the dentist but he violently shakes his head at the suggestion.

"*Si riposi,*" he says. "*Ritorni la prossima settimana alla visita di controllo.*" (Rest yourself. Return next week to have it checked.) The young woman who assisted him during the procedure sets up the appointment. He has no receptionist.

My recovery is as gentle as a summer breeze. Once the Novocain wears off, I take one Motrin before going to bed, and another in the middle of the night. I sleep fine, pain free and back to normal the next day.

Meanwhile, throughout all this, I've had time to think about my relationship with Rich. Walking back and forth to town and taking the bus to and from the hospital allowed me to consider my options. I wanted to tell him I am tired of constantly reliving what is basically the same problem over and over again, like the movie *Groundhog Day*. Then it occurs to me that this is exactly what my self-righteous ego wants – to give up, to play the blame game, to be the victim, the pseudo-martyr. My higher self, on the other hand, wants, nay, *requires* me to work it out once and for all. Ignoring the problem means I'll have to go through this again and again, if not with Rich, then with someone else, until I get it right. The alternative is spending the rest of my life in abject loneliness. Although, I am scared to death (mostly about what I'll find out about myself), I know that if we don't talk about it we'll live out our precious time in Italy as polite strangers. How tragic would that be?

The discussion turns heart-rending as we each come to trace our hurtful behaviors to situations we either experienced or observed as children. I am shocked by how much I've hurt him, never imagining how much power I had over his feelings. As we talk he repeats, for what? the hundredth time? the thousandth? … his resolve to never allow his wife to berate him. When the full impact of this hits me, I think my heart will split in two.

I'm back at my computer once again, taking in the achingly beautiful scene outside our bedroom window. Rich and I are good now. With my pride bubble burst, my world is back in alignment because Rich and I are back in alignment.

Suddenly an exquisite creature, a kind of moth they have here in Italy that looks and acts like a hummingbird, flutters over the petunias. When it throws its body into a blossom, all but the sound of its wings disappears. My heart still aches, but it's the good ache that's borne of pure beauty.

The infection in my mouth has been extracted – and I pray the infected part of our relationship has met the same fate. ♡

Update: In the U.S., oral surgeons typically house the same kind of 360-degree X-ray machine the Italian hospital has. In the part of Italy where we live, there are no specialists for extractions and root canals, so dentists make use of the specialized equipment available at the hospital. This is a less convenient way to provide dental care, but it is also less costly. The extraction of my tooth cost 100 euros. ($125)

17

DRIVING SCHOOL

Every day, as we walk the main street to do our errands, Rich and I pass the Bacchi Driving School.

"Isn't it strange that we never learned to drive a stick shift?" I ask. "I mean, we're the oldest of the baby boomers."

"I've always wanted to know how to drive a 'four on the floor.'" Rich says.

I laugh, the phrase bringing up memories of the Beach Boys and the little old lady from Pasadena.

Since most Europeans drive a stick shift, automatics are hard to come by, especially in traditional Città di Castello. Besides, renting an automatic in Europe costs considerably more.

"Hey," I say. "Why don't we take lessons here?"

"Yeah, let's do it. The few people we know who drive a stick in the States wouldn't want us practicing on their cars."

I add that I doubt American driving schools even teach it anymore.

We enter the unlit Bacchi Driving School which has model cars displayed in the front window. A tall man with a narrow nose and a brush cut emerges from a back room. He stands straight as a soldier, arms at his sides, behind an empty glass display case. We tell him, in our limited Italian, that all we want to learn is how to drive a stick shift; we already know how to drive. He tells us we must wait to speak to the owner who is in Perugia.

Our second stop at the school yields a similar result, only this time the tall man with the narrow nose says the owner has a fever. We express our sympathy and leave. Our third attempt is in the morning and the tall man with the narrow nose tells us the driving instructor will be in later in the afternoon.

On our fourth attempt, after five o'clock, we find the door locked and no sign of life inside. We read the hours on the door and sure enough, the establishment is supposed to be open at this hour.

"Poor fellow," I say of the owner. "Must still be sick."

The following evening, around seven, I stop in without Rich and find myself enveloped by a group of teens filling out forms and scheduling lessons. No adult, other than me, is present and so I wait. No one looks at me. I feel invisible. Even though the teenagers of Città di Castello are especially courteous, the longer I wait the more I don't feel like speaking Italian in front of an audience. I often mispronounce or blurt out the wrong word and although the Italians are very forgiving, I'm not in the mood to embarrass myself yet again.

The sixth attempt, in late afternoon, when, according to the hours posted, the driving school office should be open, finds the place shuttered.

Signs in Italy baffle us. The most confusing one is the *Aperto* (open) sign hanging above another sign that says, *Ferie*, (on vacation.) Which of the two signs has someone forgotten to take down? Was the store really open when the owner decided to lock up and take two minutes to run across the street for a coffee – a likely scenario – or is he really on vacation?

The seventh time we drop in the Bacchi Driving School a woman named Elisabetta sits behind a desk at the back of the room, beyond the empty glass counter. A small neat stack of folders sits in front of her.

Elisabetta appears friendlier than the tall man with the narrow nose. I think it might be easier to get her to schedule something for us, or perhaps, she might even be the instructor. She tells us we need an Italian driver's license after living in Italy for one year. We explain we've only lived here a few months and, besides, we only want to learn to drive a stick shift. After a lot of talking back and forth and still not making ourselves understood,

Elisabetta spots a friend of hers walking past. She runs out and, taking her friend by the elbow, steers her inside. The woman is from Poland but speaks Italian and English and is a willing and friendly translator. I momentarily consider kidnapping her because she not only speaks English, but also speaks Italian slow enough for us to understand. I want her to be our guardian angel for the rest of our stay.

While we are all busy getting things sorted out, the tall man with the narrow nose enters. He stands wide-legged at the front of the shop, arms folded with his back to us, staring at the people strolling by.

Once Elisabetta understands we haven't lived here all that long, she copies information from my passport and Michigan driver's license. She asks when we'll be available for our first lesson. Would morning or afternoon be better?

At that moment I look up and spot the driving school's car parked outside on the far side of the cobblestone street. It had not been there earlier. I look at it again, then at the man standing at the window when suddenly my mind connects the two. Ignoring Elisabetta's insistent "morning or afternoon" questioning, I ask who the teacher is. Both women turn simultaneously and point to the tall man with the narrow nose.

I sputter and, after a few false starts, finally manage to explain to the Polish woman that that man sent us away over and over again. Elisabetta, not understanding, keeps pressing for a time when we are free to take a lesson. Meanwhile, the tall man with the narrow nose glances over his shoulder at us and wordlessly slips outside.

I move toward the door, Rich following, while saying to the women in English and Italian that we'll have to think about it. Out on the street, the driving instructor jumps into the school's car. As he drives off I see him glance at us in his side-view mirror. I wave *arrivaderci* to him and smile. He sticks his arm out the window and waves back, a sly smile crossing his face.

I loop my arm through Rich's and as we walk home we recall the man's list of excuses: "Gone to Perugia," "Has a fever," "Not here," "Come back in the afternoon." I tsk-tsk-tsk and Rich wags his head with each revelation.

Obviously, the tall man with the narrow nose didn't want to be bothered with foreigners. Instead he did the best thing he could think to do, which was to keep making excuses in the hope we'd give up and go somewhere else – there are other driving schools after all.

That's how we come to meet Sandro – another 40ish man with a crew cut. He wears a bright orange sweater and red-framed glasses. It is refreshing to see someone with another color on besides black or brown. Blacks and browns are the colors of choice in winter. We easily schedule a lesson for the next morning.

I ask to go first to prevent myself from chickening out. With Rich in the backseat and me in the driver's seat, Sandro speaks softly and calmly using broken English. I return the favor by speaking broken Italian to him. It works well enough except for one problem due, primarily, to an idiosyncrasy my brain has: when learning, the first thing I'm told is the thing I will always remember. Tell me someone's name is Sharon and then say, "Oops, I meant to say Karen," and Karen will be Sharon to me forevermore.

With Sandro the idiosyncrasy is a bit more problematic. All I can say is, it's a good thing he has a clutch and brake on the passenger side. Before we take off, he begins the instruction. In English, he says to press "down" on the clutch slowly and "up" on the clutch quickly. Placing my left foot on the clutch and slowly pushing it down and pressing my right foot on the brake, I put the car in first gear, ease up on the brake and let the clutch up quickly as instructed. Before I can get my foot on the accelerator, the car leaps forward like a frog and abruptly dies. As it continues to rock to and fro, I look at Sandro. He looks at me. He says, "I mix up English words 'up' and 'down.'" Too late. Ears heard, brain recorded and no amount of cramming in different information can extricate the newly absorbed "facts."

Then there is this other idiosyncrasy I have – I'm scared to death of speed. I've stopped at the top of ski hills I've determined are too steep for me to traverse, taken off my skis and walked to the bottom. Even worse, I've walked my bicycle down long, winding mountain roads in Vermont. People smile at me and say nothing when I tell them this. I explain the brakes were wet and weren't stopping the bicycle properly and they continue to smile and keep silent.

During the driving lesson, I'm not sure if I can slam on the brakes in case a cyclist or a car pulls out in front of me. On top of that, Sandro keeps saying, quietly and calmly, *"Piano, piano,"* which I understand to mean "floor," as in the first floor, second floor, etc. When he continues to repeat it, I start to suspect the word *piano* has more than one meaning. I know he's not talking about the musical instrument, because the Italian word for that is *pianoforte*, which literally means weak/strong. While searching my brain for what else *piano* might mean, I lose track of my speed and coming next is a curve. I beg him to translate *piano* at the same time he slows the car with the controls at his feet.

When my half-hour lesson is up, I pull to the side of the road, stop and put the emergency brake on as instructed. Sandro springs from the car, lights a cigarette and sucks on it like a starving baby. With each inhale he gazes up at the beautiful hills surrounding us, wistfully speaking of how much he loves to drink the wine that comes from those hills. I think it is people like me who drive instructors to smoke and drink.

When it is Rich's turn and I am in the backseat with my dictionary, I look up *"piano"* and learn that in addition to "floor," it also means "Not so fast." So, in effect, when he was saying *piano, piano*, he meant "slow down, slow down."

For the second lesson Rich is handed off to a different instructor who speaks no English and I get Sandro all to myself. I suppose he didn't have enough cigarettes to handle both of us in one day.

This time, much to my horror, Sandro directs me to drive inside the walls of Città di Castello. The narrow streets make going fifteen miles per hour feel more like forty. Pedestrian, motorcycle and bicycle traffic enter and exit my path willy-nilly. The cars parked every which way on either side of the street don't help either. Weaving around these obstacles, I suppose I look like a normal driver to the Italians.

I'm not into the lesson ten minutes, white-knuckling the steering wheel at the ten and two positions, when Sandro asks my permission to smoke. He can't even wait the half hour until the lesson is over? Having quit smoking a mere eighteen months earlier, I hesitate a second before answering. I want to say "no" because

People park every which way.

I don't think it is fair for him to have one when I can't. Then I remember my well-being sits at his feet – the clutch and a brake. It is important that his concentration be tip-top and I remember how smoking always seemed to sharpen mine. I not only grant him permission, but insist he smoke.

Rich is much more conscientious about learning to drive the stick shift than I am. He not only takes a third lesson, but also practices the next time we rent a car before friends arrive from the States. We take the rental to a hilly country road and I give it a half-hearted try while Rich really works it. His practice pays off because he's quite proficient at it now.

In a pinch, I could drive the stick as long as I didn't have to go past third gear. I swear I would've taken another lesson and practiced more, but honestly, I feared I might have to take up smoking again. ♥

18

THE LANGUAGE

Twice a week Rich and I attend a language school called *Lingua Più* (pronounced *LEEN-gwa-pew*, only one hundred times faster). Literally, it means "tongue more." Don't blame me for the literal translation – that is but one of the fuzzy obstacles blocking our understanding of Italian. Its structure is backward to our way of speaking (e.g., Into English cannot be literally translated the Italian language.), with the subject most often appearing at the end of the sentence. I'm not just talking about adjectives popping up after nouns as they do in Spanish (e.g., "She wears a dress red."). I'm talking about how "Dick and Jane ran up the hill" becomes "Up the hill ran Dick and Jane."

Not so ironically, I suppose, this upside-down phenomenon with the language closely parallels my life lessons over the past four years. Everything I thought I knew for sure is its opposite and, even more incredibly, all the opposites make more sense than the so-called "truths" I learned growing up.

For example, I used to think miracles happened to us, like winning the lottery or being spared in a car wreck. Now I believe a miracle is simply a shift in one's perception.

Such a miracle occurred two years ago when I quit smoking after clinging to the habit for thirty-five years. I'd tried every which way to quit, but it wasn't until I prayed for the *willingness* to quit that all the right people and products came together to allow me to do so. Before this, smoking was my life force (I know this is hard to grasp for anyone who has never suffered an addiction). A tectonic shift had to occur in my mind (in other words, a "miracle") before I could see that quitting meant happiness instead of depression.

During the dozens of times I'd tried quitting before, I'd always get past the physical symptoms of withdrawal (one month) only to have them replaced by feelings of self-righteousness and sacrifice. *Look how good I'm being.* This always led to a depression so deep that the choice became to spend every day of the rest of my life miserable or to go back to smoking. The choice was always clear. Once my perspective shifted, the feelings of sacrifice and depression vanished. Pouf!

Coming to Italy and watching people live in a way I'm not accustomed to, is showing my perfection-seeking German-Lithuanian mind a multitude of things. The most natural behavior in my upbringing was this: It is always necessary to make order out of chaos. Much to my surprise, chaos is not always something that requires taming (my hair, of course, being the exception). In some cases, chaos can supersede orderliness in terms of effectiveness. For example, when listening to Italian, if I try to literally translate the words, I only hear the words and have no comprehension. If, instead, I relax my brain, allowing the words to enter as the chaotic jumble they are (rather than how I'd prefer them to be), I'm more likely to understand their meaning. It's really not hard to understand Italian – what's hard is relaxing enough to accept the chaos.

To the untrained ear of English speakers, it sounds as though Italians take a lot longer to get to their point. The more I learn Italian, the more I know they *do* take longer to get to their point. Imagine if you only had one word to cover all of the following: granddaughter, grandson, niece and nephew. If I tell you I saw my *nipote* the other day, which could mean any of them, it stands to reason that it will take me an additional sentence to explain which of the four relatives I am talking about. (Side note to Italian speakers: It is impossible for people new to the language to pick up the "il" or the "la" – to denote gender – before "nipote.") This explains one reason

Italians talk so much – they need to. Another reason is that unlike English, Italian is so ROUND, so flush with vowels that sail into the air like soap bubbles, who can blame Italians for loving to hear themselves talk?

I suspect the talking gene in Italians is more fully developed than Rich's and my inherited ones from Eastern Europe. He and I can walk the river path to town and not speak to each other for ten to fifteen minutes at a stretch. This happens even when we're not mad at each other. Whenever two (or more) Italians pass us, they are *always* talking. Whenever two (or more) Italians pass us on their bicycles, they are *always* talking. When Rich rides his road bike up twelve percent grades with Italian friends, so high on a mountain the tops of their heads risk scraping the sky, the Italians are *always* talking. The rule is, where there are two or more Italians, there is talking. An exception *may* be church. If there are other exceptions, I have yet to witness them. Sometimes I'll notice a hush in – no, not in the library – but in high-end restaurants. People still talk, only in subdued tones, with exceptional reverence, no doubt in deference to the food. No nation's citizens could love and revere food more than Italians.

The same goes for Italian birds. I am *not* kidding! They chirp more in Italy. They chirp more in the morning and more as the sun sets. I know because I've actively listened to birds in many regions of the United States.

Here, there is a bird who sits in a tree and sings all night. It is not a nocturnal bird, it is a songbird, and its repertoire could match any Italian opera. We hear this bird every night as we climb into bed, and I hear its delightful warbling every time I get up to go to the bathroom. No matter what time of night it is, this bird is singing. Rich and I lie in bed wondering what that goofy bird's tree-mates think. Still, we have no trouble sleeping.

Then, much to our horror, one night we don't hear him, and Rich says, "I hope he's all right." Oh, for crying out loud. His worry means I'll have to walk to town just to "Ask Jeeves" about it on the Internet.

After asking Jeeves, I learn that only the "bachelor" songbird sings at night, and will continue to do so until he finds a mate. We miss that goofy bird singing at all hours, but we also wish him every happiness with married life.

Anyway, I chaotically digress. Rich and I usually arrive early for Italian class at *Lingua Più*. We couldn't be late if we tried. It's not in our genes. Since we're early we often stop in the coffee bar next door to the school, both located in a strip mall. There, we sit and enjoy a cappuccino. We've usually eaten oatmeal and fruit for breakfast before leaving home, so the coffee is simply a nice treat. Two times a week we go there, and my astonishment at what I witness every time never abates. I watch, as one after another person, from teenager to centurion, walks in, crowds around the bar and drinks (or more likely gulps) an espresso (while standing) and stuffs a pastry into their mouths. This is their *entire* breakfast.

If I had a sweet roll every morning, it would, first and foremost, make me fat, which, by American standards, most Italians are not. Second, it would make me sick to my stomach and, third, I'd feel faint and famished well before the Italians break at one o'clock for their three-hour lunch. If, as a nation, they've nurtured an ability to have a sweet roll and coffee for breakfast without any negative side effects, is it no wonder they are such a happy people?

Time for class. Rich and I are the only students in the one-hour class. For a while we had another man, a Briton, which not only brought down the hourly rate but spread out the humiliation. Roberta is our language "therapist" who I sometimes think of as our language "terrorist." In reality, she is as sweet as the pastries eaten in the morning: petite, fortyish with light brown eyes and long curly blonde hair that makes her body look even tinier. Her heart-shaped face reminds me of an angel. This committed vegetarian wouldn't hurt a flea.

She always comes to class prepared and on time, is knowledgeable, fluent in English, and never forgets her sense of humor or her deep affection for and curiosity about people. She is so dedicated that, despite our urgent protests, she often continues to teach beyond the hour we paid for and not charge extra. Despite all this, and having completed all our homework, we have never arrived for class feeling confident. And we always leave with sweat stains stretching from our armpits to our waistbands.

We spend weeks learning reflexive verbs. Part of my pleasure in Italy is that so many of the verbs *are* reflexive. Wait! Don't skip to the next paragraph. This is not about grammar. When a verb reflects back on itself, it means the person doing the action is responsible for the verb's action. For example, in Italy, as a matter of course, you wake yourself up, wash yourself, dress yourself, comb yourself, lift yourself up from a chair, etc. True, it can be argued that someone else can comb the hair of another person, for example, but those actions are not reflexive.

Then there are what I refer to as the metaphysical reflexives that raise philosophical questions, such as "to cut oneself" (why does one cut oneself?), "to place oneself" (why would one place himself, for example, in a compromising position, or in harm's

Roberta of Lingua Più.

way?), "to tire oneself" (at what point is the choice made to overdo it?), "to lose oneself" (is it pride or something else that prevents the stopping "of oneself" to ask for directions?). While most reflexive verbs have their non-reflexive counterpart (i.e., "I cut myself." – reflexive, or "You cut me." – non-reflexive) the verb "to shame" is *only* reflexive. In other words, in Italy, no one can shame you but yourself. I like that. My favorite? A person does not get bored – a person bores himself!

Lera Boroditsky, a psychologist at Stanford, is gathering evidence to see if language shapes thought. From my observations of the Italians, I'm sure the outcome of her studies will clearly show a relationship. The fact that the Italian language assigns each noun as either feminine or masculine makes everyone more sensitive to gender here; thus the women are more likely to walk with their hips thrust forward and the men with their chests thrust forward. The sentence, "She broke the cup," is more likely to be viewed as breaking itself among Italians, whereas Americans are more likely to say, "*She* broke the cup," blaming the "she" for the exact same action.

Since a thought precedes every action, imagine how these types of thoughts carry over into the day-to-day lives of Italians. We know, after experiencing a dreadful winter in Italy, that these people are not happy solely because of their reportedly uninterrupted resplendent weather. It rains here. It gets cold here. It snows here. These people, at least in our small town, don't go around blaming anything on anyone. The impatience level is so much lower than ours I sometimes want to stop and take their pulse.

Say, for instance, the stoplight turns green and the person in the car at the front doesn't move immediately? No honking. Cars parked every-which-way? Others understand; they've been in the same situation. A customer takes out his or her wallet *after* their groceries have been tallied? No one in line rolls their eyes.

Even more delightful, no one seems to worry about lawsuits. At Macrì Country House there is an in-ground swimming pool with no fence around it, no lifeguard, and no one to keep non-residents out. The owners openly invite non-residents to come over and go for a swim, even when no one is there. It makes them happy to share their good fortune and to see people having fun. None of the residents, who pay extra for the pool, get their nose out of joint because they have to share the pool with non-residents.

People don't seem overly possessive about their property either. I explore many roads that dead-end on someone's property, and no one says a peep, much less comes out of their house with a shotgun. And farmers here do own shotguns which they use to hunt. Once, when I was on an exploration, a farmer came out of his house as I was walking on what assuredly was his property. I didn't know what to think, what to do or what to say. The old fear of being yelled at choked me into paralysis. Hesitation worked in my favor. On the way to his tractor he simply wished me a good day *(Buon Giorno!)*. More trust, less fear. Less fear, less attack, mentally and physically. All of these attributes contribute to more love.

As everyone knows, there are so many things in Italy about love – even the graffiti written on the municipal bathroom walls sing *"Ti amo!"* *"Ti amo!"* ("You I love!" "You I love!" – See, they even say "I love you" backward!). I've had occasion to read every bit of graffiti on each of the two stall doors, and there is not one word of attack on either one of them. (Yes, my dictionary goes everywhere I go.) *"Ti amo"* is written on benches, trees, walls, guardrails, motorcycle windshields, baby buggies. The words are ubiquitous.

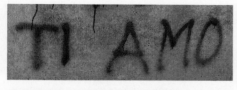

On a guardrail.

On a bench.

A heart outlined in green chalk on a sidewalk in the "Green Heart of Italy."

None of this keeps Rich and me from attacking ourselves. We continue to expect to come to Italian class speaking and understanding perfectly. Never mind that there are fourteen different verb tenses in Italian to English's measly six.

Because of this self-imposed anxiety, every time we go to class at *Lingua Più*, we rent a DVD afterward to watch in the evening instead of studying (we study one to two hours the other five days a week). In effect, we have to salve ourselves with a cappuccino before each class and salve ourselves with a movie and homemade popcorn (shaken in a pot over the stove) after class, which illustrates just how expensive language lessons can become. We've been told, and have read, that at "our age" this daily brain aerobics is worth every euro. We sure hope so because our children are going to inherit a lot less because of it.

Despite ourselves, we keep the faith. *Some* day we will stop "talking" Italian and start speaking and understanding it. Rich's faith doesn't falter because he's never given up on anything. My faith doesn't falter because I believe in miracles, and speaking Italian fluently is going to require one. ♥

19

TELEVISION

One of the "benefits" of living in a non-touristy town is that we don't have access to any English-speaking television programs. Large cities, such as Rome and Florence, televise CNN or BBC news, but not Città di Castello. We tell ourselves this no-holds-barred language immersion is good for us. It would be as easy to fall into the habit of watching English-speaking programs as hanging out with English-speaking people. Life in this small town leads us not into temptation and puts the kibosh on spending a lot of time in front of the tube.

There are two things we watch regularly though. First is the news, not only because Rich and I are both news junkies, but also because we'd been told that watching TV helps people learn a new language. This would be true if the Italian TV production staff focused their footage on things more directly related to their stories. Although there are a variety of ways camera people can shoot a story, the technique preferred here is to first focus from a distance on a door or window of a building related to the story and then, as the narration proceeds, to slowly zoom in on it. Granted, the doors and windows in Italy are far more impressive than those in America, but whenever the narrative gets long winded, looking at a door or window for two minutes doesn't assist our learning.

For the most part we know the topic being talked about, but we miss the details. We knew, for example, when Pope John Paul II, referred to in Italy as *Il Pappa*, was not feeling well, but we couldn't decipher the problem or prognosis.

Every time they showed Pope John Paul II, he was sitting in front of a window (for he knew that was the only way the cameramen could find him) and, without fail, the window was always open, letting in cold, dank wintry air. I, probably along with every mother watching worldwide, kept shouting, "Shut the window, for heaven's sake!" but, as is often the case, no one listens.

With the exception of the Pope, it doesn't matter what else is on TV – world politics, sports, game shows, soap operas, commercials – every program involves young, attractive women. Most are brown-eyed brunettes; a few are blue-eyed blondes. Some wear scanty outfits while others wear business suits that plunge to their navels or are, at the least, sleeveless. The sight of two anchors, a man and a woman, sitting side by side at their news desk always makes me chuckle. He's old, gray-haired, pasty-looking and wears a rumpled suit, shirt and tie. She's young, beautiful and showing enough skin to make the viewer shiver either with cold or lust.

Notwithstanding the window and door videos, a few of the news stories are much more graphic than America's coverage. If someone is rescued from the water, Italian TV not only broadcasts the rescue, but also the resuscitation attempt. If the attempt fails, they show the body bag being lugged to an ambulance. Whenever an Italian soldier dies in Iraq, we see his casket and are told a story about his life. It doesn't matter the rank of the soldier – each one receives three days' coverage.

The weatherman doesn't spend ten to fifteen minutes yammering about cold fronts, warm fronts and predicting what's going to happen throughout the week. In fact, he doesn't even attempt to forecast beyond the next twenty-four hours. The weather report lasts about twenty seconds, sometimes less. Glance away and I miss it. A map of Italy is flashed on the screen with one of four symbols pasted on top of each area: a sun, cloud, raindrop or a snowflake. Although cold and warm fronts are also shown, an assumption is made that viewers understand one from the other and don't need a nightly explanation. If something truly unusual is coming our way, a uniformed military meteorologist gives the report without fanfare.

The second broadcast we watch regularly is a game show called *L'Eredità* which means "inheritance." Contrary to its title, though, contestants on this show don't inherit any money, they earn it. To win, they have to be smart, poised and have a little luck. The show begins each evening, Monday through Saturday, at 6:30, 6:35, 6:40, 6:45 or 7 p.m. – times vary for no apparent reason – starts with six contestants and concludes with one by process of elimination. The one-and-one-half-hour show, give or take fifteen minutes, carries only two commercial breaks of four minutes each.

We enjoy the show because it is one of the few we understand. The questions are printed at the bottom of the screen. We can read many of them. Some, especially those pertaining to America, we can answer.

The show includes true-and-false, multiple-choice, and a round of rapid-fire questions. At the end, there is a *Who Wants to Be a Millionaire* type of format with the final contestant. This allows us varied opportunities to hone our language skills. Add to that all the banter in-between questions, plus the time allowed contestants to put their two cents into exchanges (even when it isn't their turn), and the show can be counted as quality language and Italian culture study time.

Not only educational, this game show is loads of fun. If we knew Italian better we suspect, judging from watching the audience, it would be hilarious. The thirty-something host, Amadeus, is a tall skinny guy with sparse skull-capped sandy-blonde hair. He has a large nose, which he often acknowledges good humouredly, and is assisted by a long-legged brunette,

Amadeus and Giovanna.

Giovanna, with perfect skin, blazing white teeth and black shiny straight hair that flows over her shoulders. Amadeus usually wears black pants, an open-collared white shirt and a black jacket with ultra-thin glittery stripes running through it. Giovanna wears a one-piece fuchsia "teddy," for lack of a better word, her midriff cinched in black leather. Her feet sport strappy high heels. Even with the outfit, she can't help but exude wholesome vibes.

Both Amadeus and Giovanna are likeable in a "Bob Barker and Janice" sort of way. I wouldn't have been surprised if there'd been something going on between them except for the fact that she wears an engagement ring. Perhaps it is their chemistry; more noticeable to Rich and me because we can't understand much of what they say to each other, but we do notice their body language.

Amadeus stands center stage with a computer screen set atop a swivel post in front of him. Surrounding him is a circle of contestants, ranging in age from 19 to 79, each standing in front of a computer screen of their own. Like Regis Philbin's *Who Wants to Be a Millionaire*, the set flashes with blue lights and background music plays constantly. The main difference is that home viewers can see the audience which encircles the set.

After the first segment of the show, when the atmosphere has grown too intellectually heavy, four other young women – Simona, Ivana, Ombretta and Claudia – cut the tension with a dance. For a one-minute interlude they shimmy and shake to rock music under pulsating lights in skimpier costumes than Giovanna's. When not dancing, they sit on the sidelines looking pretty and laughing at everyone's jokes.

If these women performed on a game show in America, I'd scream "bloody sexism," but somehow it seems perfectly natural in Italy. Perhaps I'd feel differently if I was at the start of my working life rather than at the end of it. Life is much less urgent and mellower after turning fifty. Besides, all women feel appreciated in Italy. Men do not discriminate – they flirt with all of them, regardless of age, class or level of attractiveness.

All *L'Eredita's* audiences hold teachers in high esteem, for all contestants who are teachers garner more applause than any other profession. The audiences also join in singing any song derived from a question. No matter if it's an old song that is played, such as *Nel blu dipinto nel blu* (which people in the U.S. often refer to as *Volare*), or a Beatles song, it is obvious Italy is a nation of people who enjoy music and have it in common with each other regardless of age.

After another couple segments of the game are completed, Giovanna, struts into the inner circle where Amadeus continues to stand, and dances to him and the camera. The dance, much more wholesome than that of the foursome seen earlier, lasts about thirty seconds and the audience stands and claps to the music. Giovanna always ends the routine by throwing kisses to the audience and saying, *"Baci, baci, baci!"* ("Kisses, kisses, kisses," pronounced BAH-chee, BAH-chee, BAH-chee.)

There's one other character on this program – I call him "god" with a small "g." We never see him but we hear him. He is addressed as *Santucci* (at least that's how my ear hears it) and called upon whenever an explanation or ruling is needed. Whenever *Santucci* speaks, Amadeus looks up at the ceiling, seemingly deeply interested in what "god" has to say. For people sitting in the audience and TV-land, *Santucci* is the educational aspect of the show.

Contestants are encouraged to be themselves, and many take advantage of this by displaying a talent or sharing a treat. Six nights a week for weeks on end, we never see an idiosyncrasy repeated. One contestant who makes pizza for his living brings enough to serve everyone in the audience. During another show, a member of the production crew is called upon to help an extremely short, pudgy, contestant whose head barely reaches the bottom of her computer screen. The crew man sweeps her up into his arms and holds her the entire time she plays the game. A woman with bright red hair proclaims her love of dance, so she takes Giovanna's place center stage that night. An older man plays the accordion while Giovanna dances with Amadeus. Organized chaos. It's no wonder the length of the show varies. In Italy, time isn't given the same degree of importance we give it.

The person most likely to win the game is the one who not only knows ordinary things, such as world geography and pop culture, but also knows trivia, including the names and stats of Italy's soccer squads. It's also helpful to know how to differentiate the hundreds of Italian pastas, cookies, olive oils, wines, operas, works of art and to have a more than passing familiarity with each of the country's twenty regions. If they don't know a *cantetta* from a *taglietta* (two differently shaped pastas), they're sunk. Whenever an art question is answered, the work is shown on a large screen which *Santucci* explains.

At the end of all television shows in Italy the credits are not scrolled from top to bottom, but crawl lickety-split left to right across the bottom of the screen. If you want to catch someone's name, forget it. Amadeus and the final contestant wave while Giovanna throws kisses and waves goodbye by making her hands mimic the beaks of quacking ducks.

By the time we finish watching the news and *L'Eredità*, our brains are fried. The rest of the evening the television sits idle. Being a bookish marm, I greet the silence with open ears. ❤

Update: On a train I happened to sit next to a woman reading an Italian TV magazine. One of the articles featured Amadeus and Giovanna, and guess what? They are both engaged – to each other. He has a daughter from a previous marriage. Two years later, I will read that they also have a son of their own.

20

CRITTERS

Thanks to my mother, I'm not afraid of bugs, and it's a good thing too, because zillions of them fly around our apartment at Macrì. I'm happy they are here, otherwise the warblers, mourning doves, swifts, swallows and martins wouldn't hang around and sing so sweetly to us.

Another thing my mother taught me was to leave spiders alone, even those in the house. Spiders are eight-legged blessings; they eat the other bugs, she said. And now, living in Italy, where there are no screens, and windows and doors are left open all day, I witness firsthand how right she was.

Spiders spin webs in corners high and low, and between the brick ceiling and the wood beams and, I'm sorry to inform, under chairs. When their building phase is over, their inert phase starts. They sit all day and all night in one spot until something gets trapped in their web. Our apartment is a deathtrap for wasps and bees. Dare they seek refuge in any of its nooks and crannies, they will be caught and eaten.

When I clean the floor, a Daddy Long Legs occasionally gets caught up in my Swiffer. (Yes, they sell Swiffers here, and I can't imagine how Italians swept their glazed brick floors before their invention.) Carefully, I carry the Swiffer to the window and shake off the spider onto the tiled roof of the apartment below. I continue Swiffing and less than a minute later something near the window catches my eye. There, on the sill, I spy one spider leg, then another, followed by a third and then I see the body of the spider I just shook out methodically climbing its way back in. I can't help laughing.

When it comes to flies, sometimes they dash in and out in a flash; other times they take a quick peek in each room before exiting as though nothing in our place holds any interest to them. It's almost insulting!

Every morning, dozens of gnats fly in, spend the day spiraling near the ceiling in what appears to be senseless movement, and then, after the sun sets, fly back outside. Once night falls, the only critters left in the house are either spiders or victims of spiders.

In May, when the temperature drops in the evening, we shut the windows before going to bed. In summer, we leave the windows open day and night and are never bothered by any bugs. A couple times we think we hear a mosquito, but we never see one, except on the footpath next to the river. If there were mosquitoes around, Rich, our resident mosquito magnet, would have large welts on his skin as proof.

Not one-hundred yards from our bedroom window is a spring-fed pond, referred to by the Italians as a lake. To the two of us, who grew up and have lived in the Great Lakes region all our lives, this "lake" looks more like a pond and sounds more like a swamp. It's not at all stinky though. At night, the frogs and toads make a ruckus reminiscent of prepubescent boys competing to see who can make the most vulgar sounds. While drifting off to sleep I can't help but chuckle at the *burbles, rips, grunts* and *screeches*, sometimes so loud I feel as though we are sleeping at the swamp's edge. Adding to the sensation of being outdoors is our ability to see the stars through the window, unobstructed by glass or screen. Each month, as the moon grows full, it spotlights Rich's face for part of the night – something that disturbs my sleep, but not his.

At the beginning of July, our landlady brings her granddaughter's four parakeets – one silver and three powder blue – from their home in town and puts them in a cage tied from a branch of a pine tree next to the parking lot. A small wooden box hangs at the back of the cage where they can huddle away from the wind and rain.

Their presence reminds me of how we used to have parakeets when our children were small. I pampered those birds so much I worried that strong cooking odors might upset them. The four birds left outside in Italy seldom have a clean cage, often spill their tray of food (forcing them to eat from the

Four generations. Our landlady Lucia, with her daughter Maria, her mother (another Maria) and her granddaughter Livia.

bottom of the cage), drink brackish water, inhale fumes as cars drive in and out of the gravel parking lot and sustain temperatures ranging from fifty to ninety degrees within twenty-four hours. And they thrive! Sometimes I can be so uptight.

Also in July, the wasps (or hornets, as some people call them) build nests in our house from regurgitated plant material. Yes, the spiders eat as many wasps as they can – probably to the point of making themselves sick – but they are outnumbered. Thanks to a little research on the Internet, we learn that it is the female wasps that have the stingers and build the houses. Once completed, they lay their eggs, close up the houses with more reconstituted plant matter and two weeks later their babies are born. The male's only job is to mate; he does not carry any weapons and lives a shorter life than the female. I dare not comment on this phenomenon for fear of serious digression.

Female wasps also build nests in the outdoor oven where I grill. They are so focused on their construction work that a blazing fire doesn't deter them from at least attempting to enter. It is annoying trying to turn chicken on the grill with wasps buzzing around my face and arm as I reach in. I'm sure the fire is equally annoying to them.

131

The wasps are crazy for making nests in the window jambs of our three windows. Thankfully, they aren't aggressive, unless someone messes with their babies (or so we've read), but still, I'm uneasy sticking my head and arms out the windows to deadhead the petunias that grace the bedroom windowsills and trail off onto the tiled roof.

We ask our landlady what we can do about this manic nesting activity. She refers us to the handyman, Paolo, who removes the nests with gloved hands. Afterward, despite the July heat, we have to keep the windows closed for a week. This prevents any newly pregnant wasps from coming in. The sad part is that it also keeps out the worried mother wasps who've already built nests inside but, unbeknownst to them, have been destroyed by Paolo. The poor things hover and cling outside the window all day, waiting for any chance to get inside to their nests and babies. It is a pitiful sight.

All in all, the invasion lasts almost two weeks.

In August, it is so hot the wasps stop coming inside. Instead they nestle in the leaves of the petunias, basil and parsley growing in pots on the windowsills. Like spiders, the wasps now sit inert all day. The plants are so loaded with them that their blackness covers every inch of green. It is an improvement over having them fly in and out all day, but their presence on the plants limits our ability to stick our heads out the window to check the temperature or to see who is at the pool. Thankfully, they leave at dusk in time for us to snip some basil and parsley to include with dinner, after a thorough rinse, of course.

On the night of the summer solstice, we happen to walk home from town long after sunset. I've taken to carrying a flashlight as a matter of course, but on this particular night a full moon makes it unnecessary. On the narrow farm road and throughout the forest glen by the creek, hundreds of fireflies wink, transforming a hill of tangled grasses into a mass of twinkling Christmas lights. As we walk up a rocky incline in the road, it feels as though we are walking through a blanket of slow-moving stars.

During breakfast, which we often take outdoors, we watch swallows and swifts dart through the air eating bugs while skimming close to the ground. In the evening, again outdoors, we watch the same birds, only this time they circle so high they are mere specks in the sky. Oddly, the swifts in town (not just in our town but also in other cities) don't act similarly. Instead of peacefully hunting for bugs, they chase each other in circles while screeching like a bunch of screaming meemies. I suspect the competition for food is higher in the cities.

Many people have dogs. Neutering appears to be *vietato* (forbidden) – my guess is Italian men can't even think about having *that* done to their dogs.

Along the river trail, many owners walk their dogs, usually unleashed. Nineteen dogs out of twenty are well-trained – none stop to greet, sniff or show any curiosity in passersby. As I cross paths with them I see their eyes steadily focus on their master or mistress. It seems to be a rule that people not talk to or pet anyone's dog without permission. Or, as my daughter observed when she visited, people don't seem to go all gaga over dogs like Americans do.

Dogs are allowed in stores and, while their owners dine, lie quietly under tables at restaurants. Since they are so well-behaved, it is as much a pleasure to see them out and about enjoying life as it is to see the wide range of ages of people mingling together. No one, not even small children, appear to be afraid of the animals.

We have heard, however, that Italians are counseled to "Be German!" when training their dogs – in other words, discipline them consistently. The Italian mentality of "live and let live," "feed others until they burst," and "have fun when at work and at play," doesn't quite jibe with the training dogs require. It remains a mystery to me – the restrained behavior of the dogs considering the giving, giving, giving spirit of the people.

"Mary" the wiry, tri-colored mix who belongs to the owners of Macrì, is a one-woman army, barking at anyone she doesn't know, sometimes snarling at their ankles. She isn't much interested in being petted or cuddled, except occasionally by Lucia's husband, Domenico. "Mary" has a real job. She patrols several acres of land, and what with new people checking in and out all the time, she has to quickly learn who has permission to be on the property and who doesn't.

At first I don't like this dog. I think she is mean spirited and that she is a he, going so far as to refer to her as "Bubba." An Italian friend familiar with the dog reinforces my belief in its meanness. When mentioning the dog, the woman's face screws up and she whispers, *cattivo* (bad).

"Mary," Macrì's guard dog.

One day I sit by the swimming pool and ponder "Mary." When new guests arrive and get out of the car, she races toward them, barking madly only to get yelled at by one of her family members. Putting myself in "Mary's" paws, I notice how seriously she takes her job – protecting her people and the property of her people. I start to feel sorry for her. I want to defend "Mary" and tell them she's just doing her job. But of course I don't.

After I change my mind about "Mary," she stops barking at me whenever I return home. No longer do I feel she's an odd sort because she doesn't run up to me wagging her tail, looking for a pat on her head as most dogs do. Accepting her as she is may seem like a small thing, but inside I feel a chunk of my self shift.

Thanks to my mother, though, I don't need to shift any of my hard-held beliefs regarding bugs. For the most part, we're okay sharing living quarters. ♥

2 1

THE FLOWERS

Almost every day we walk alongside myriad fields to get to town and, being city folk, can't identify one plant from another. We know the area is known for growing tobacco, so we suspect some of the fields are tobacco, but which ones, we aren't sure.

In the spring, the field directly in front of Macrì sprouts what looks to be grass; we guess it might be sod to start lawns. A week later we discover that the "sod" is really wheat...yes, a form of grass, but still. Sometimes I'm thankful I don't speak the language well. What if I had asked the farmer, "So how's your 'grass' coming along?"

When I was a preteen in the early 1960s, I used to collect wildflowers at our lake house during the spring and summer. Because I'd read Rachel Carson's newly published book *Silent Spring*, I limited myself to one flower of each kind to use as a model. I'd sketch and color it, identify it with the help of a library book, and write its common and Latin names underneath. Then I placed it in a used mayonnaise jar to enjoy until it withered. Okay, so I've never been the life of the party, but I sure was happy.

In Italy, with spare hours for the first time since youth, I rediscover the hobby; only this time there isn't any need to pick even one flower thanks to the invention of the digital camera. I can practice micro shooting until the cows come home and not waste one bit of film.

I must confess, though, that one day I couldn't resist picking a large handful of red poppies. In the spring they are ubiquitous; even growing between railroad tracks and guardrails next to the highway. It didn't take me long to find out why there are so many. Five minutes after I put them in water, they collapsed over the side of the jar.

Each month displays more of Italy's abundance. In May it is wisteria, the fragrance fermenting in the sunshine until it intoxicates us. After a rain, their boughs drape so low over the footpath they reach the ground, causing a wet obstacle course for pedestrians like us. Bluebells, asters, coral geranium, violets, grow wild, and in people's gardens, irises and the first bloom of roses.

In June the jasmine perfumes the air in town, and at night it wafts through our bedroom window. In the fields, the shiny yellow petals of buttercups complement the poppies.

It seems that everywhere I've ever been in my life, be it next to the highway in Italy or in an alley in Detroit, I always see reminders of my failure to grow hollyhocks in my own backyard. I thought it might be because there wasn't enough sun in our yard, but every summer day in Italy I pass one sturdy stalk of pink hollyhock, a double-petaled one no less, growing under a pine tree where no sun reaches it. Every time I pass it I am torn between sticking my tongue out at it and admiring it.

It is the beginning of July, though, that brings me to my knees.

One beautiful summer morning, we crest, for the hundredth time, a hill overlooking a field of what had been, up until then, mystery plants. When I catch sight of what they are, I stop stone still except for my jaw dropping. There, standing ramrod straight before us, which the day before looked like two-foot stalks of who-knew-what, are hundreds of five-foot tall, fully blossomed sunflowers! Since the day we arrived in Italy, not once did I leave the house without a camera, and this day is no exception. But so overcome by the sight of these "beings," and trembling with excitement, I can't think straight to hold the camera steady. As we continue into town we see field

upon field of sunflowers, oohing and aahing as if watching Fourth of July fireworks.

Italians call sunflowers "*girasole*." *Gira* means "it turns" and *sole* means "sun." When I'd heard sunflowers face east and turn their heads to follow the sun as it rises in the sky and then turn toward the west, I pictured how the girl's head in *The Exorcist* turned. Uh, not so for the sunflowers. I keep a close watch on them for a couple weeks and do see some of them turn their heads *in an attempt* to follow the sun, but their heads only turn a tad. A few of them are especially cute, tilting their heads back with their chins up, like Rich does when he suns himself.

Before going out to take the digital photos, I reread the camera's instructions. For me, this is a once-in-a-lifetime shot. In the field, the flower heads nearly reach my chin. Between the height of the plants and their "faces," I find myself not only personifying them, but playing with them. Their very presence encourages my latent playfulness. While aiming my camera at the backs of their heads I tell them, "Don't turn around," and I picture their shoulders shaking with giggles. I think my constantly talking to them means I am going bonkers, until I am walking with Rich and I clearly hear him greet them "Hello."

When photographing them, they often sway in the breeze. The instruction booklet had warned about "difficult subjects" who move the moment you snap their picture, but I never once imagined until now a sunflower being categorized as a "difficult subject." Every day, when I crest the hill, I break into a grin as if my best friend had just greeted me on the path. For two weeks, they smile back.

Then the rains come. Their heads bow, as if in prayer. With time, they bend over more, like old ladies with humped spines. Their petals turn from sunny yellow to dull black. They stand like that for many weeks.

Then, in the fall, the farmers' machines make one quick pass, unceremoniously decapitating them. I stand and gaze at the field of headless stalks, transfixed between the memory of their glorious, sun-fed beauty, and the desolate reality now before me. The sense of loss is palpable. I had danced with these "beings"; together we had raised our faces to the warm sun and lowered them against the biting rain. They taught me how to be a child again ... and now they're reminding me of how everything ends ... everything except memory and love. ♥

2 2

MID-TERM EXAM

In the middle of summer we feel so much gratitude for the many
people who've touched our lives that we start to plan a thank-you party. We
want to invite the three young women we'd met from the real estate offices,
our Italian teacher, our Rotarian friend Giuseppe and his wife, his close
friends Quinto and Liana, cyclist Giordano, his wife Clemenza and their
teenage son, my hairdressers and their preschool son, and all the residents
at Macrì. The residents include one man from Argentina, one from Italy,
one woman and her daughter from Slovakia and two men from Israel.
Of course we'll invite our landlady, Lucia, and her husband Domenico,
and perhaps we can hire their daughter Maria to cook since they own a
restaurant on the premises. Our gratitude is as long as our list of invitees.

We enlist Mario, who lives below us, to translate a meeting with Lucia.
She gives us cost estimates. Before we can even get back to our apartment
to crunch the numbers, the buzz about the party has reached everyone
at Macrì. Sadly, we can't afford to provide dinner for that many people.
It upsets us knowing how much our neighbors would have loved a party.
I worry our relationships with them might cool as a result, and there's
nothing I value more than being okay with everyone. Ai yi yi! Now what?

We scale back the idea of a dinner party by renaming it a pool party. It
would be held in the afternoon, and we'd pay Maria to prepare finger foods
and order in pizza.

We return to our landlady with our translator in tow. Both Mario and Lucia think the idea is ludicrous, though they tell us this much more kindly. I don't think they grasp the concept. They argue it is too hot in the afternoon to have a party. Yeah, right, I think. Never mind that everyone who stays at Macrì sits around the pool on weekends from eight in the morning until five in the afternoon. What is even stranger is that they bake under the sun all day and never get into the pool, saying it is too cold. To us, Lake Michigan is cold; the sun-drenched pool at Macrì is tepid.

The idea dies. Moreover, we realize it would be next to impossible to get everyone, other than our neighbors, to come on a weekend.

In the end we decide to take a new tack; we'll handle each group individually. For Giuseppe, Nerina, Quinto and Liana, we'll throw a dinner party. We want more than anything to prepare and present a perfectly splendid evening for these people who've been extraordinarily generous to us. Neither couple would dream of describing a dinner hosted by Rich and me as a mid-term exam, but for us, it is. We feel compelled to serve a Grade A dinner and to show them that we were good students under their tutelage and learned the Italian way of entertaining.

Rich and I spend many happy hours planning the menu, shopping, cleaning, and cooking. We write out a detailed timeline. We even factor in studying Italian a couple hours before their arrival so as to attune our ears and mouths for the conviviality to come. We yearn to show them – who have been patient with us beyond reason – that our Italian has, indeed, improved.

Everything will be done Italian style, starting with the arrival of the guests at 7:30. The *apertivo* will be a drink of chilled, non-alcoholic *Crodino* since one of our guests no longer drinks alcohol. Dishes of peanuts and olives will be set out. The *anti-pasto* will be slices of cantaloupe draped with the special Italian ham *prosciutto*. For il primo, Rich will make his from-scratch mushroom risotto – an Italian rice dish that requires a lot of patience and stirring. *Il secondo*, will include both *pepperonata* – a side dish of cooked red peppers, onions and tomatoes – and grilled *Chianina* steaks, the prime of the prime. *Dolce* will be ricotta cheese coated with sugar and topped with slices of strawberries, whole raspberries and blueberries. Espresso coffee and chocolates, followed by a choice of after-dinner liqueurs, *vinsanto* or *limoncello*, which Italians say aid digestion, will complete the dinner. We allot the standard three-to-four hours to savor the food and friendship.

We prepare the setting (my favorite part): a freshly ironed yellow-and-white cotton tablecloth thrown over a table situated under two large canvas umbrellas on the patio overlooking the swimming pool and the wheat fields with the Apennine mountain range in the distance; a candle, protected from the wind by yellow canvas; and a side table for extra dishes draped in prettily patterned oilcloth. A potted cactus bursting with fuchsia-colored flowers decorates one of its corners.

Much to everyone's relief, after several days of 95-degree temps, Mother Nature blows the stifling heat away providing a resplendent, refreshingly cool evening.

Liana and Quinto arrive first, accompanied by their sweet yellow lab mix, "Deke." They climb the stairs to our apartment. Quinto ties "Deke's" lead to a banister outside our door at the top of the stairs. Liana offers me a gift so lovely I nearly weep when I first catch sight of it. In several shades of gold, the embroidered design on the long table runner sports the insignia of the city of Città di Castello. When I look at it my throat tightens with gratitude. To keep from crying, I need to look away. If someone had asked me earlier in the day, "Is there anything in the world you want?" I would've been hard put to think of something. But here it is, an outstanding example of a craft I enjoy doing myself, right here in my possession, representing, in all its glory, the place where Rich and I have settled.

Giuseppe and Nerina, two of the most outgoing and happy people I've ever met, arrive soon after, bearing wine to go with dinner. The two glass bottles they hand us still have "virgin olive oil" labels on them. This means that at the end of the last grape-pressing season, Giuseppe had procured a quantity of wine from a grower who poured it into the emptied and cleaned olive oil bottles Giuseppe had used throughout the year and saved for this purpose. How's that for on-the-spot recycling?

With all of us seated around the large wooden table in the main room of our apartment, sipping *Crodino* and popping peanuts into our mouths, the party is well underway.

Rich had thought ahead to pull out the photos of a trip we'd taken with his eighty-five-year-old mother and sister when they came to visit us in Italy. Giuseppe, always fast on the uptake, picks up the half-dozen photos and starts a conversation about them, showing them to the others. When the conversation dies down several minutes later, Giuseppe pulls a small plastic Italian flag from the inside pocket of his jacket and a felt-tip pen. He autographs it and passes it around the table for the others to sign. This, too, touches me. It's as though he's made us honorary Italians. As Rich eases the stick of the autographed flag into the pot of basil on our windowsill, I ask, "Do the flag's colors really represent tomatoes, basil and mozzarella cheese?" and they all laugh.

We head downstairs and outside to the brick patio overlooking the pool while Rich prepares the *anti-pasto*. I had set out a bottle of carbonated water, the kind preferred by most Italians, and a pitcher of water I'd drawn from the tap for Rich and me. We often see Italians drawing water from artesian wells into plastic water bottles, but have yet to see them drink water from the kitchen faucet, which we do regularly in the States and in Italy.

Giuseppe teasingly suggests the water in the pitcher be replaced by the wine he's brought but when I move to do just that, he waves his hand and shakes his head; no, not really necessary. He is right though. That would've been the Italian way.

Our landlady, Lucia, who has known our guests since they attended the same elementary school in Città di Castello, walks across the parking lot from her restaurant and visits awhile with our guests. Meanwhile, two families who live in other apartments at Macrì kindly vacate the pool area in deference to our party, and put together their own party on their porch near the outdoor oven at the rear of the house. I sense, with relief, that there are no hard feelings about the previously discussed "everyone included"

party that had to be aborted
before it even got off the ground.

Lucia's dog "Mary," Macrì's
guard dog, causes a bit of a stir
with "Deke" who is leashed to a
nearby railing on the patio. After
a few minutes of chatting, Lucia
leaves, her dog following, and
we sit down to eat. Rich hardly
finishes half of his *anti-pasto*
before it is time for him to start
the laborious process of making
the *risotto*.

Conversation flows at the
dinner table for about twenty
minutes, and then our guests start

Nerina and Giuseppe.

asking where Rich is. I tell them he is making risotto, and they nod with
understanding, Giuseppe pantomimes tedious stirring and we all laugh.

I hear someone mutter the Italian idiom
for "never ending" – it's called "building a
cathedral," which in some cases took 500
years. They all settle back and engage in the
kind of conversation only close friends can
have and I watch with pleasure. Every now
and again one of the women kindly tells
me in simple and slow Italian what they are
talking about.

Another fifteen minutes pass, and again
they ask where Rich is. I excuse myself,
check on the fire. I had laid it earlier in the
afternoon and lit it right before the guests
arrived. It looks as though it's ready for

"Deke"

the steaks. So soon? I toss some more wood on it and go upstairs to our apartment to see Rich putting the finishing touches on the risotto. We take it down together and everyone applauds as Rich comes into view. Again, he spends only a few minutes eating, then rises to start grilling the steaks.

Twenty minutes pass. It is dark now and the temperature is dropping. Everyone pulls on the jackets they'd brought, all accustomed to the valley's cool evenings.

Suddenly, a waitress from Lucia's restaurant appears at our table with a platter. She sets it down with a flourish and a smile and quickly disappears into the night. I lean forward to see what's on it. Two steaks. Our guests dig in, Nerina noting the steaks are too rare for her taste. I slump back in my chair, scratching my head. The steaks look too thin to be the ones Rich told me he'd bought. No one questions that it was Lucia's waitress who delivered the platter. I am afraid to say anything because I'm not sure what is happening and don't know enough Italian to question anything. I wonder if Lucia might have sent the steaks from her restaurant kitchen as a gift to her old-time schoolmates. Or maybe Rich had seen the waitress and enlisted her help to deliver the steaks while he cooked the other two? Or had he asked Maria, the restaurant's cook, to prepare two of the four steaks in her kitchen to help speed things along? I catch Giuseppe's eye and say in Italian, "I think these are from Lucia's kitchen," and he nods.

The tea candle on the table has spent itself and it is darker on the patio than I remembered from previous evenings. Looking over my shoulder, I see that the floodlights which usually illuminate the area around the pool haven't come on. I excuse myself to get another candle. On my way upstairs, I stop at the outdoor oven and ask Rich if he will cook one steak a little longer since Nerina likes hers well-cooked. He says "sure," as I watch him turn a steak over. The steak is at least two times, maybe three times, as thick as the ones being eaten at our table. I ask him if he'd enlisted Maria to help him cook a couple steaks? I can't keep the worry out of my voice. When he says no, I tell him how two steaks had been delivered to our table by the waitress. Rich turns away from the oven and looks at me, his face as questioning as I know mine is.

When I return to the
table with a new candle, I
note that, in my absence, an
additional two steaks had
been delivered. My paralysis
in saying anything worsens.
What if our dear landlady,
who has given us all manner
of foodstuffs since our arrival,

The forno where the steaks are grilled.

was being her usual generous self? Sure the steaks weren't of the grade
Rich had bought, and my less sensitive self might've complained about a
gift not only of inferior value but that also messed up our well thought-out
plan. The new me, though, the me who lives in Italy and is learning to not
take everything so seriously, decides it is more important in this case to be
nice than to be right – a concept that hadn't even entered my mind until I'd
reached my fifties. Always the slow learner.

With the exception of a portion of meat our guests had saved for Rich,
the steaks are devoured. When Quinto comments again on Rich's absence, it
occurs to Liana to joke, "No wonder Rich is so thin. He never eats!"

I excuse myself yet again and take another peek at the outdoor oven.
This time Rich isn't there. Not only is the wood burned up but the embers
appear to have lost their heat. Upstairs, I find Rich busy cutting the four
thick steaks into pieces, putting a well-done piece aside for Nerina. I
tell him, a little too bluntly, "Forget it, our guests are, for all intents and
purposes, finished eating."

Going with the flow, he puts down the knife and fork and opens the
fridge to take out the ricotta for dessert. I love him for his unquestioning
flexibility.

"I'll take one steak out in case someone is still hungry," I say. "We can
save the rest."

I run down the steps and out the door. What I see makes me stop short.

Standing between our door and our neighbor's porch, are Lucia the landlady, Maria the cook, and the waitress. All six of their hands are cupped over their mouths, Maria's face red with embarrassment. Our neighbors sit silently around a table on the second-story porch. Suddenly it all makes sense. It had been our neighbors – partying on

The second-story porch where our neighbors partied. Not pictured: The stairs up to our apartment on the right.

the porch in the back – who had ordered the steaks from Maria's kitchen. The waitress had delivered the steaks to the wrong group! I scurry over to where Lucia stands, hand her the plate, hold up my forefinger and say, *"Un momento!"* Turning, I run back up our stairs.

Much to Rich's shock, I tell him, as calmly as possible, that we need two more of the beefy steaks he's cooked – one for our guests, in case they are still hungry, and one to give our neighbors since our guests had inadvertently eaten the ones they'd ordered.

Outside again, I hand over another plate to Lucia to give to our neighbors on their porch and everyone seems happy. I return to our guests seated next to the pool with a plateful of the steak Rich cooked. Setting it before them, I explain – in truncated and, I'm ashamed to say, screeching Italian – what had happened. By some miracle they understand me and simultaneously clap their hands, throwing their heads back in laughter. Polite people that they are, each tries a bit of Rich's steak and judge it far superior to the earlier ones. Being understood, I think, is one of life's biggest blessings.

Not two minutes later, cook Maria arrives at our side table where the leftover portion of steak for Rich, who has yet to eat, sits covered by a plate.

Without saying a word, she lifts the plate and starts forking the steak onto the platter she holds. I stand and touch her arm. When she looks at me, she leans over and nervously giggles into my ear, "The other people ordered four steaks." My goodness, I think, the two we gave them equaled the four we got from your kitchen! How dare you pilfer more! I am so aghast I can't speak English much less Italian.

When Rich finally arrives with the desserts, our guests applaud him again for the fantastic dinner, and we all eat the sugar-coated ricotta with fruit, lightly sprinkled with espresso.

After dessert, I take everyone's orders for espresso. Two want caffeinated, two decaffeinated and two pass. When I leave to prepare the coffee, everyone is happy to spend some time with Rich and I feel the weight of making conversation, in Italian, lift from my now stooped shoulders.

When I return with the coffee and a small bowl of tin-foil wrapped chocolates, the lights in and around the pool pleasantly illuminate the patio. I also notice that Lucia has pulled a chair up to the table and is chatting with our guests while "Mary" her dog sits on her lap. More shocking, to me, at least, is that Lucia's husband, Domenico, sits in what had been my chair, and Rich is holding "Deke's" lead tight as the dog strains to reach Lucia's dog. I think, *"Che serà, serà."* With the labor-intensive part of the dinner over, all we have to do is relax and enjoy everyone enjoying each other. Had I foreseen the future, I would have accidentally on purpose fallen into the pool just to end the evening then.

One of the neighbors who'd been partying on the porch, lets his dog "Leo" out of his apartment and unleashes him. "Mary" starts barking. The Dalmatian immediately races pell-mell into the darkness. The owner shouts, "Leo! Leo!" Meanwhile, "Deke" scrambles under the table, eyes searching for "Leo," and when he rears up in an attempt to escape and join the shenanigans he lifts the table off the ground. In the making is a potential avalanche of candles, wine and dishes. All the while, "Mary" continues to bark her head off. By this time, Rich has had to dig his heels into the patio brick to restrain "Deke."

Despite the racket, Domenico continues to talk to his old friends, gesticulating, as Italians do, with a cigarette in one hand. At one point he interrupts his story and offers everyone at the table a cigarette. Suddenly, it is the 1950s and I am a co-star in an Italian movie. I want a cigarette in the worst way, and would've taken one had I not continued to sit dumbstruck, sticking with the same mode I'd been in since the first steaks arrived at the table.

Domenico's cell phone rings. As he takes the call I cop a longer look at him. His silver mane of hair contrasts nicely with his dark olive skin and his bright white teeth. He looks both casual and crisp at the same time in his three-piece suit, tie and starched white shirt. He becomes so engrossed in his conversation that he stubs his cigarette out in the bowl of foil-covered chocolates. I'm sure he thinks it is an ashtray. When he finishes the call and takes up where he'd left off with our guests, I surreptitiously pull the bowl toward me, salvage what chocolates I can, place them on the table, and push the empty bowl back toward Domenico, for which he thanks me in the gentlemanly way he has.

Sitting there, still hungry myself since my nerves had made off with my appetite even before the party began, I look down at "Deke" who now sits at Rich's feet looking exhausted and dehydrated. I think about getting him some water from upstairs and then I think, what the heck ... I take the pitcher of water from the side table and lean down for him to drink directly from it. Domenico continues to talk.

I wonder if the night will ever end. It is almost 11:30; our guests have been with us for four hours, and the air has turned nippy. They are starting to fidget. Nerina is wearing capris and sandals and though she is bundled up with a warm jacket, she appears to be shivering. I rise to get some lap blankets from our apartment and excuse myself. By the time I start back down the stairs with two throws over my arm, our four guests and Rich are coming up the stairs carrying the dirty dishes. Without planning it, the action of my getting up helped break up the party.

The two couples keep saying how sorry they are that they didn't get much time to talk to us, especially Rich. To get them to stop apologizing, I ask, my voice probably still on screech level, "Did everyone have a good time?" to which they all nod vigorously. I say, "Then that's all that's important." With that we all kiss one another on each cheek, and Rich and I walk the four of them down to their cars and bid them goodnight.

While doing the dishes Rich and I try to sort out the evening. I can't stop laughing as we review one thing after another. He agrees the preparation of the risotto "took longer than I thought." I point out that over three decades of marriage the phrase "it took longer than I thought" has lost every ounce of its charm. He also agrees the risotto was too salty, and I ask him how that happened since he'd made it so perfectly before. He says that when we first came to Italy, he couldn't read Italian very well and had put in only half the bouillon the recipe had called for. This time he followed the recipe precisely and it turned out too salty. I also concede that I should have fed the fire more. The steaks would not have taken so long to cook had I done so.

The next morning, Sunday, while eating breakfast alone outside by the pool – Rich is riding his bike with Giordano and 200 other people – it occurs to me that the waitress, the cook Maria, and her father Domenico kind of messed up our dinner party. For a minute I consider whether something should be said. Then I recall all the mistakes I've made with the language and the culture and how Italians not only don't get the least bit perturbed by my errors, but few even bother to correct me. It becomes clear that blaming anyone for anything would be fruitless, especially since nothing was done with malice. All of us were doing the best we could at the moment, and our relationship with our landlady's family is far more important than making a stink about an honest mistake.

So, did we pass the mid-term exam? We think we did, with flying colors. We did what most any Italian would have done in similar circumstances – we laughed. We knew that's what Giuseppe, Nerina, Quinto and Liana were doing, and we knew the six of us would recall the evening over and over again with each other and laugh even more about it. Our relationship with the two couples and the owners of Macrì had become one where blame and guilt did not exist. If that isn't heaven, I don't know what is. ❤️

Update: I am happy to report that our other "thank you" get-togethers with friends were unremarkable.

23

LEAD AND PIPE

Thanks to the Internet, I can continue to take jobs editing while in Italy. I even have a favorite bench on which to edit – it's in front of a fountain with an angel on top. Printing the manuscripts is the tribulation.

Even though there are seven printers in seven separate locations in Città di Castello, a city of 38,000 inhabitants, the problem is that only one printer works. The others have dried-out ink cartridges, aren't connected to the Internet properly or are broken. The hours of the Internet Point where the printer functions seamlessly are limited, its six computers almost always occupied, and it is the most costly of all the places. In Italy, this situation of having almost everything needed to complete a job is known as a "lead-and-pipe situation." At least that's what our Italian friend Luigi calls it.

Luigi is not only a great chef but also a great storyteller. Granted, the story I'm about to recount doesn't come close to the entertainment value it would have if you heard it straight from Luigi's lips. The gist of it, though, is important in that the words "lead and pipe" can be used as shorthand to describe a common Italian situation.

There are three guys, a Swiss, an Italian, and an American. All three die at precisely the same moment, and thus end up knocking on St. Peter's gate simultaneously. St. Peter opens the gate, strokes his beard and, looking down at them, shakes his head.

"What?" asks the man from Switzerland. "What's the matter?"

"I'm afraid none of you can enter heaven at this time," St. Peter says.

"Why not?" asks the man from Italy.

"As you already know, you've done some things in the past that weren't exactly, uh, how shall we say, virtuous. Therefore, all three of you must spend some time in purgatory before entering heaven."

The three huddle for a moment and come to the conclusion that St. Peter is right.

The American, first to break from the huddle, says, "Okay, where is purgatory?"

St. Peter points his forefinger in a fair-to-middlin' position – somewhere between heaven and hell.

The three set off to purgatory where they find a corridor of doors, each with a different country's name on it.

"Let's go to Switzerland," says the Swiss. After knocking, the door opens and inside the threesome sees white hot flames dancing about and hears wailing and screaming emanating from behind the doorman. "What is going on in there?" asks the Swiss.

"Ah, that," the doorman says, indicating with his head at the raging hell behind him. "Here we stick hollow pipes down people's throats and pour red hot lead through the pipes." A look of horror crosses the faces of the three men until the doorman says, "You might want to try another door."

They brighten, and the American says, "Follow me. Everything's better in America." The other two men follow him to the door marked "USA" on it. When it creaks open, they see a scene similar to the one they'd seen in Switzerland's purgatory. "What goes on here?" demands the American, shocked that things don't look any better.

"Ah, that," the doorman says, indicating with his thumb the raging hell behind him. "Here we stick hollow pipes down people's throats and pour red hot lead through the pipes."

The Italian yanks on the shirttails of the Swiss and American men and says, "Let's get outta here. Let's try Italy." As the three men stride off, the

American doorman yells, "It's the same thing everywhere you go."

The Italian knocks on the door marked "Italy." When it opens, the eyes of the three men widen. They see green pastures, sunshine, flowers, puppies playing in the grass, people picnicking. All three are shocked, not to mention skeptical.

"Where are the hollow pipes and hot lead?" asks the Italian.

The doorman replies with a shrug, his arms outstretched, palms skyward, "You shoulda know how itta works here. One day no pipe, the next no lead. What we do? We wait."

That's what Italians do. They wait. Patiently. And they laugh. That's what I am learning to do here. So accustomed was I to getting an idea in my head and seeing it through before bedtime that it comes as a shock that I can wait, sometimes up to a week, to cross something off my to-do list. The funny thing about these obstacles is that they often bring me in contact with new people. Several months in, and Rich and I know enough people here to say hello to a half dozen of them on a walk through the historic district.

It saddens me to know that the youth of Italy are moving more and more toward our way of life when we should be leaning more toward theirs. It's easy to become accustomed to the convenience and comforts of America, but I fear that in time, as we Americans retreat more and more into our increasingly impersonal culture, that we will eschew the connectedness that gives us health and flavor. After all, it's not always a good thing to have lead and pipe available on the same day. ♡

Update: What is inexplicable to me is that I can't pack up this patience and bring it home with me. The moment the plane flies over the American border I revert to the Type A, "give it to me now or someone will get hurt" mode.

24

The Tobacco Factory

When my children were in grade school, they played a game I'd never heard of. Every time we passed a cemetery, they held their breath until our car cleared it. As I understood it, the children's grapevine deemed that if you inhaled while passing a cemetery, the ghosts would sense your life and suck the breath out of you.

I need to adopt a similar game on my daily walks to and from Città di Castello. A tobacco-drying factory, which only operates in autumn, sits next to the farm road I trek daily.

As a former smoker, I'm shocked at what happens when I smell nicotine emanating from that factory. The first sensation is pleasure – ironically, fresh and unadulterated – such as the one smokers experience with the first one or two cigarettes of the dozen or two they smoke each day. (For those who've never experienced this addiction, the majority of cigarettes smoked are not smoked for pleasure, but to maintain a so-so comfort level.)

While walking past the processing plant, the smell of tobacco leaves drying becomes so powerful on my second inhalation, my brain buzzes into nirvana. I imagine, with great relish, what it would be like to smoke again. How easy it would be to simply keep on walking past Macrì Country House. How quickly I could reach the little bar in the hamlet of Lerchi and buy myself a pack. Ah, how wonderful that first cigarette would be!

Like an alcoholic, though, I know I can't have only one. Just because I haven't smoked in two years doesn't mean I'm no longer addicted. I am.

And I always will be.

Returning to it would be sentencing myself to hell on earth. Even though I know this would be stupidity of the highest order, still, there is that moment while walking and inhaling when I seriously consider it.

Once I pass the factory, I breathe regular air again, and all desire to resume smoking dissipates. Often I'll walk the remaining quarter mile home before it occurs to me that my craving vanished. It's a weird phenomenon.

***

We have a new neighbor, a young woman. She lives in one of the apartments connected to ours in the rehabbed farmhouse. Unlike our previous neighbor, she smokes. Somehow her secondhand smoke makes its way into our apartment. I don't give it any thought until today when I go to pack for a three-day side trip.

As soon as I open a small suitcase on the bed, indecision grips me. I pace back and forth between our bedroom and the guest bedroom where I keep my things. Rich, who sits reading in the living room that separates the two bedrooms, watches me with furrowed brow. I glare at him.

Why the sudden mood change, I wonder? As much as I dislike packing, I can usually breeze through a ten-minute assembling session.

Before long, I'm crouching in front of my armoire crying, paralyzed and unable to make a decision about what to pack. I recognize my feelings as those of withdrawal. I'm going through it all over again. When I become conscious of the sound of my sobs, I swallow, stand up and pull a tissue from my pocket. As I'm blowing, I remember the young girl next door, and the smell of her smoke.

I rush from the bedroom. It is time to pinpoint where the smoke slithers in. I enter each of our four rooms and sniff. The odor is strongest in the bathroom. I flip the switch off. A sliver of light emanates from a teeny-tiny opening surrounding the wood beam where it connects the young woman's bedroom and our bathroom's shared wall. Thankfully, the space is so small I can't see through it into her bedroom, and I assume she can't see into our bathroom.

I call our landlady on my cell and ask if she can come over. She's not far away. She's in her restaurant across the gravel parking lot from the farmhouse. I want her to smell the smoke herself. While waiting for her, I consult my Italian dictionary to learn how to tell her I'd quit smoking and how the smoke from the next apartment bothers me. When she arrives, she listens patiently since my Italian is truncated and not easily understood. In the bathroom she assesses the situation and agrees that the leakage is unacceptable. Within the hour, she sends her handyman over to fill in the crack.

With my brain back to normal and all irritation gone, I start packing. While folding a pair of slacks I try to remember how many times I'd tried quitting. Too many times to count. I do remember, though, that the last time – the quit-forever time – didn't come until I stopped praying for the *willpower* to quit and started praying for the *willingness* to quit. Once I asked for willingness, ideas flooded my head, helping me form my own treatment team. The combination of all these "angels" working as a unit created the miracle I needed to overcome the addiction. I'm not saying I quit without discomfort. It entailed the pain of withdrawal which, at the time, I thought would last forever.

But here's the kicker: In the end I didn't have to "give up" cigarettes as though I were sacrificing something. Suddenly cigarettes, which for decades I'd *perceived* as my best friend, always there when people failed me, became the breath-sucking demons my children so feared when they passed a cemetery.

Now that I understand the "game," I hold my breath each time I walk past the tobacco factory. ♥

25

THE YEAR COMES TO A CLOSE

I'm writing this with only two weeks left to our 11-month stay in Italy. Time wise, it's a great place to be. Though we're still here, we know we'll soon be seeing all those in America we miss so much. I look forward to going home for another reason: the temperatures here are stalled in the 30- to 50-degree range, and it's been an extremely foggy, wet and snowy November. Soon I'll be home where it doesn't cost so much to heat our house to "cozy."

Once there, I'm sure there will be things I'll desperately miss here, such as the daily surprises. Why, just a couple days ago, while walking past Piazza Garibaldi I did a double take. Much to my delight, a 1700s-style carousal had been erected in Piazza Garibaldi. During the day, this masterpiece is wrapped tight in canvas but, as darkness grows,

The view from our kitchen window during November. That's the swimming pool down there. The mountains have been erased from the skyline.

around 4 p.m., it's unwrapped and lit up and starts its everlasting journey of circles accompanied by upbeat music. Its luminescence serves to further contrast the November gloom, with two tiers of horses, feathered plumes sprouting from high, proud heads. There are more theater lights around the carousel than I can count. A few hours from now, by 7 p.m. it will be filled with children while parents, grandparents and townsfolk sit on nearby park benches or stand in huddles, socializing. Remember, it's November, it's around 40 degrees, and it's before suppertime. Not everyone's at home watching television.

This phenomenon reminds me of when we first arrived in January. It was snowing giant wet flakes, and it got dark early and it was easy to feel bored and bummed out, wanting to curl up on the couch under a blanket and say, "Wake me up when this is over." Instead, we bundled up and crossed the street in front of our

1700s-style carousal had been erected in Piazza Garibaldi.

then-apartment and entered the medieval walls. We decided a cappuccino would warm us up and headed for one of the local bars. Sopping wet from the snow, we ducked inside only to run into a standing-room-only crowd, drinking all manner of beverages, laughing and joking. I could smell the steam rising from wool coats. The atmosphere was warm and splendid and fun, and we didn't even know what they were laughing about. We were welcomed with nods and smiles, with *Ciaos* and *Buona Seras* and felt the goodwill, warming us even before we took a sip of cappuccino. In the small towns of Italy there is an energy we can only feel in the hearts of big, vibrant American cities, like New York and Chicago. Connectedness is so much easier to access here and I know I'll miss it once we return home.

The other thing I'll miss about Italy is the dirt. That's right, the dirt. I'm not a big fan of dirt, but I now know it's not the evildoer it has been made out to be. My German and Eastern European roots make me yearn for order, cleanliness, and the American Way. In Italy, people don't care if a tree is "dirty," dropping ugly green pods on the ground that, when it rains, turn to something accurately resembling bird pooh. They don't care if their local trains haven't been scrubbed, ever. Oh, the Italians like to say their trains are "cleaned" regularly, but I would hasten to add that "cleaned" is not the correct word. The correct word is, "picked up," as in "picking up the house." Picking up is a far cry from cleaning.

On a recent train trip the seats and aisles overflowed with people so we had to stand for four hours – squished next to one of the exit doors. I ended up sitting (and thankful, I might add) on the dirty step everyone steps onto to get on or off this train that, trust me, has never ever been "cleaned." I saw with my own two eyes the years of filth accumulated on the door handles.

In the train's bathroom, the flap at the bottom of the toilet bowl was missing. You could see *terra firma* freewheeling underneath. Nice breeze on a hot day. Saints help you if you drop something you didn't intend to drop!

What amazes me is that despite all this dirt – on the keyboard at the Internet places, in the airtight cubicles where we made phone calls after dozens of people had done the same thing before us, I haven't caught one cold or suffered any flu bug. The only thing to befall me this year was an infected tooth, and I've already explained that mystical malady.

You might think I've washed my hands regularly. Not true. And even when I do, there's never anything but cold water in most restaurants and public toilets and rarely is there soap.

The farm road to town gets a little slushy in November. I wear waterproof galoshes that slip over my shoes and, right before I enter town, I ditch the boots behind a clump of bushes. It is guaranteed that NO Italian is wearing boots anything like mine.

The other mysterious thing is that I have yet to see someone with a cold. Smoker's cough I've heard, but colds, the runny, sneezy, sniffly thingamajig we usually get doesn't seem to attack Italians – at least the Italians I've come in contact with. Maybe all the sick people stay home like they're supposed to, listening to their bodies and resting them rather than "pushing through the pain" only to go out and infect the healthy.

After seeking warmth in sunny Greece for a week in late October, we returned to fungus growing on the inside of our bedroom walls. We asked our landlady about it and good old Paolo came over and examined this black stuff creeping next to where I put my head at night. His verdict? We'd been away for a week and the house hadn't been aired out during that interlude. Never mind that it's

Our bedroom at Macrì.

been raining wet noodles for days – the wettest November in some fifty years we'd heard. Even the waterfall behind our bedroom window is roaring again as if it were spring. Crocuses, popping their colorful heads up through the earth, think Easter is around the corner. We're enjoying yet another crop of bright-yellow dandelions, the only cheeriness breaking the gloom. And

The footpath in winter.

the dry riverbed we need to cross on the farm road to town is now ankle deep and all our trusty stepping stones have drowned.

There's no bathtub in our country house apartment and a hot shower doesn't heat me through like a good soak does. Most nights of our entire stay here (even in spring and fall when the temps fall at night), I don't wear pajamas, but a sweat suit. Charming.

In addition I had to drink a glass, a full glass, of wine to rid myself of the chill that had settled inside my bones just so I could sit at the computer and type this, I'm wearing long underwear, two sweaters (one of which is 100% Italian wool) and a jacket. Never mind that we've been keeping the thermostat set at 59 degrees because heat costs so darn much and wine is so much cheaper. Never mind that it takes five days to dry the laundry. Try that with one set of bed sheets.

First you have to wash the sheets and pillow cases (remember the "short" two-hour wash cycle?), then hang them outside for five hours, retrieve them before it gets dark, a cloud bursts or a bird poops on them, then iron them over and over and over again with a bath towel draped over the marble-topped dresser. The resulting steam only serves to feed the weeping walls more moisture, until we can scrape the fungus off with a knife! But hey, we're not sick. Maybe all this damp will kill us later, but right now we're doing fine, thank you very much.

I try to see the good in both sides of the issue: America's penchant for sterilization, and Italy's tolerance for dirt, but I can't. Both sides have gone too far. I'd prefer my landlady to cage her chickens rather than allowing them to poop all over the place, including in front of our door, but, on the other hand, I'm glad she doesn't waste time and money and pollute the land trying to rid the expansive lawn of dandelions with weed killer.

And now I know I was wrong and judgmental when we first arrived and

Rich's homemade surprise puts a positive spin on an otherwise crummy day.

I went out and bought a new doormat. The one that was there looked tacky beyond belief, so I bought a brightly colored one and threw the old one out. Now, six months later, I notice how tacky beyond belief the new one I bought looks.

I hate to admit it, but my 100% German-American mother was right. "Moderation in all things," she used to say. Americans should stop obsessing about germs and Italians should give them a bit more thought.

I'll agree to the "moderation" clause – right after I've had a chance to get home and enjoy a ridiculously long hot soak in the tub. 💕

26

THE FOLLOWING SPRING

We fly from Rome to Detroit in mid-December and stay put for four months, happily ensconced in the cozy warmth of gas forced air surrounded by friends and family.

But we can't leave well enough alone. We decide to return, during some nice-weather months, mid-April through mid-July. (We would stay longer, but we want to be home for the birth of our first grandchild, and I really need to get back to work.)

We know we can never duplicate the previous year, and we don't try. One can only live the moment.

And it is in just such a moment that my world flips upside down – not in a tragic way, but in a way dramatic enough to make me question whether I'd made any progress in my personal growth during the previous year.

Once again we live at Macrì in the same apartment. We reconnect with everyone, and make good use of the pool. I walk regularly to and from town and Rich bikes frequently.

With two months down and mid-June to mid-July to go, my wake-up call arrives.

It happens on one of those resplendent Italian mornings, while walking alone to town on the farm road that my right foot rolls over some stones and slips out from under me. Slammed to the ground before I can even think about catching myself, pain shoots up my leg. It reminds me of the

The farmer's house is at the top of the hill. The fall happened around the bend to the right and up another hill.

many times I've sprained my ankle before ... in Maine, Iowa, North Carolina and Pompeii, Italy.

Okay, I think. A week out of commission and I'll be good to go. But when I crane my neck and twist my torso to look at my ankle, I nearly go into shock. My foot angles weirdly to the right. The sight of it roils my stomach. I try to straighten it, to no avail. My foot hangs off the end of my leg like a puppet's.

I've walked this road hundreds of times; in fact I've walked my entire life and never broken anything. I've taken calcium supplements for years and done aerobics for decades in order to prevent this very occurrence. I try to deny the reality of what has happened, but the fierce pain won't let me.

Rich is cycling up in the mountains with a couple other guys this morning. We are both doing the things we love most to do in this beautiful area of Italy. At least I was doing what I loved up until a few seconds ago.

Since I've fallen right below the crest of a hill, I scooch myself to the side of the road for fear a car (rare as they are on this stretch) coming over the hill won't have time to see me and I'll be further humiliated by being crushed to death.

I yell, *"Aiuto! Aiuto!"* which, as you might imagine, means "Help!" I know there is a farmhouse over the hill and people are always home there.

After a few minutes of shouting I am encouraged. The farm's two dogs come into view and, seeing me, hesitate about getting too close. They run wide circles up and down the edges of their property while barking their cute little heads off. I talk to them as if they are both "Lassies"

"That's right girls, go get someone! Good girls!" It won't occur to me until weeks later that maybe they would've gotten someone had I spoken to them in Italian. Sigh.

Meanwhile I lay back and take in the beauty of the trees arching over me, and listen to the nearby waterfall and the birds singing – oh, how they sing here! Did I mention the day is resplendent? I wish I could lie here all day, but that darn pain keeps interfering with my reverie! Besides, I am getting tired of holding my leg up – can't let the foot touch the ground – too wobbly ... and even more painful than allowing it to dangle.

Once I determine my shouts are being heard only by the dogs, I take out my cell phone, a contrivance I've pretty much eschewed up until now. Who to call? Not Rich – he is miles and miles away – on a bike. I'm not far from where we live, so I consider calling our landlady, but I never understand her Italian. Besides, she doesn't drive. And in this crisis I doubt I'd be able to understand Quinto or Liana. Restaurant owners Nadia and Luigi speak English and Italian as does our Italian teacher, Roberta, but I don't think they're familiar with the area where I've landed. I've shown this road to our American friends, Peter and Marsha, but they flew back to the U.S. yesterday. Giuseppe and Nerina are in Bologna.

I look through my cell directory and remember how last year the efficient, non-Italian side of me had locked in the emergency numbers of police, fire and ambulance. No, the number is not 911, and yes, there is a different one for each department.

I call the ambulance and explain the situation in Italian. *"La mia gamba è rotta."* Explaining where I am located is another matter altogether. My location isn't so much remote as it is unknown. (I took the "road less traveled" and see where it got me!) While talking to the emergency operator, the dogs get braver and circle closer to me. The less timid of the two, the beige-colored one with floppy ears, comes right up and takes a few laps at my forehead and then scampers away. That would've been cute had my leg not been broken.

I try to wait for the ambulance with patience by taking in the scenery and, most important, restraining myself from looking at my foot, or thinking about the pain in my leg. Thanks to Girl Scouts, I've taken enough First Aid classes to know that the most important thing you do for someone who may go into shock is to reassure said person. So, I enlist Mother Nature and her divine power of peace and harmony to keep reassuring me. Damn, she's good!

Then I hear the siren! I hang on to the thought that once I'm found, the worst will be over. (How naive we can be when in the depths of despair!) I can tell the ambulance is on the evil highway and I hear it pass me, which is the best way for it to enter onto the road where I am trying not to writhe since writhing only makes the pain worse. But then, instead of hearing the ambulance come toward me, I hear it go up into the hills. Darn it anyway!

I call the ambulance operator again and explain to the lady that I hear them but they are going the wrong way (turns out I had said the road I was on was *"accanto a"* – "next to" – a landmark, when indeed I should have said the road was *"davanti a"* – "in front of" – said landmark.) The woman reassures me they will find me, both she and I not realizing my mistake. Finally, the ambulance driver calls my cell, and I must've got my words worked out for within a minute I hear the ambulance wheels crunching gravel above me at the crest of the hill. Thankfully, he is driving slowly and stops short of crushing me.

Out of the ambulance jump three people: A large, muscular, bald-headed man; a fresh-faced, beautiful, young, slim, dark-haired female; and a young man with a wood-bead rope necklace around his neck and straight hair cascading over his forehead. God, they are beautiful, and not because they are my rescuers. They are *really* beautiful, all three of them, outfitted in their neon orange bib overalls and white long-sleeved shirts and, from my perspective on the ground looking up at them, set against the green of the treetops and the blue of the sky. I must restrain myself from whipping my camera out of my purse and snapping their photo. I want to share their beauty with everyone.

They strap me to a board and heft me up. I reach out for my purse lying forlornly in the road. They tell me not to worry, but I worry anyway. *Everything* is in there.

I finally see the old farmer, the one I'd been yelling to for over ten minutes. He stands next to the ambulance with his arms crossed, watching me being loaded in. I suspect he is as deaf as a corncob.

Someone retrieves my purse.

On the drive to the hospital the bald man drives and the young woman starts an IV. The young man with the beaded necklace asks my name and if I'm allergic to anything.

Despite my controlled voice, both my legs shake uncontrollably. In an attempt to grasp the woman's hand for moral support and to steady myself, I lean forward. She reaches toward me, but too much space separates us. Besides, she, too, is having trouble keeping her balance in the shifting ambulance. The road has so many curves I try to grasp onto the ceiling in an attempt to keep my leg from moving. It's no use. There's nothing to hang on to. Shift to the left. Ow! Shift to the right. Ow ow!

Eight miles later, we arrive at the hospital where I commence to scream as they take off my shoes. I scream when they take off my khakis, yelling in Italian to "Cut them! Cut them!" They ignore me.

My screams settle into moans and groans during the EKG, but in X-ray the screams start again as my leg is first placed one way and then the other. The sounds of my screams reverberate off the walls. Suddenly I become aware of my screaming and I listen to it. The sound is horrific. I bite my tongue.

After the X-rays, I'm pushed back to the emergency room. As I listen to the doctors discuss what to do with me, I learn the fall broke my tibia and fibula near my much-abused ankle. When I pick out the word "*intervento,*" I am stunned. Of all the worries I worried while lying on the ground, I'd never worried about needing surgery. Fearing I might be too anesthetized or groggy to call Rich later, I decide to call him now. I had hoped to let him finish his ride, but it's only eleven o'clock in the morning.

My phone call catches him during lunch break since they started riding at six a.m. The concern in Rich's voice is palpable. As he continues to say things, such as, "I can't believe it! Are you all right?" I hear his voice catch. I pooh-pooh his concern and admonish him to pull it together and listen. I do this because it is the only way I can keep *myself* together.

As it turns out, all the operating rooms are spoken for. I need to wait until the following morning. The doctors tell me they will fit me with a temporary cast. I ask if it will hurt and they all shake their heads, "No." I look to the nurse standing behind the doctor holding my leg. While nodding her head up and down, she puts a finger between her gritted teeth and pretends to bite down on it. As the doctors work, I stuff a wad of sheet into my mouth and bite down like I'd seen in Westerns when a cowboy is getting a bullet extracted.

Afterward, as I'm being wheeled out, I thank the nurse profusely. Soon I arrive in a two-person room where the other patient, a kind-looking young woman, is waiting to be released. Her husband sits on the foot of her bed.

A nurse comes to my bedside to remove the empty bottle of IV painkiller. Still in agony, I ask for another. She says I can't have another one so soon. How long until the next one? I ask. When she says four hours, I yell at her in what I think is the Italian imperative to call the doctor *pronto*.

Within minutes a young doctor stands at my bedside. I tearfully explain in Italian that I had fully expected the worst of the pain to be over once I arrived at the hospital. I don't know where my much improved Italian comes from. I'm using tenses I'd only glanced at and never studied. The doctor nods while I speak articulately but ponderously, and he looks properly concerned during my drawn-out plea for help. When I finally finish, he asks, "So, woulda you lika some morphino?" Oh, for heaven's sake! He speaks English!

After he leaves, I try to deal with the pain plus my overall physical discomfort. All I'm wearing is a sweater and a pair of underpants. Everything else had been removed for the EKG and other examinations. Since I am on the west side of the hospital and it is hot in the room, despite most of the "hurricane" shutters being rolled down, I ask for a hospital-issue smock. After asking four times, and being ignored four times, my roommate informs me I am to bring my own pajamas. Oh, if only I'd thought to pack them this morning, I think with the sarcasm pain so effectively generates.

Having to urinate, I tell a nurse, *"Devo pipi,"* literally, "I have to pee." She promptly brings me a bedpan and a roll of toilet paper. An hour later, still unable to pee while lying on my back, I try to sit up a bit. Any slant, I reason, will help get the flow going. While hoisting myself onto my elbows, I pull out the IV and bleed all over my sweater and the sheets. I buzz for a nurse who puts in a new IV, changes the sheets and, at long last, gives me a hospital-issue gown. Given my irritation, I can't restrain myself from yelling in English as she walks out, "Aha! I knew you were holding out on me!"

Suddenly my leg is in dire pain again. I start to cry but try to hold back since my roommate is about to be released and her husband is sitting on her bed, and there's no curtain to draw between us, and there are no tissues. I pull a few squares from the toilet paper roll, but the tears keep streaming silently down my face and neck. Soon I am pulling large sheets off the roll. My roommate gets out of bed, rustles around in her bag, then comes over and offers me a purse-size package of tissues. She is so nice.

After she is discharged and I'm alone, I try to console myself that Rich will be here soon. Instead, I break down and sob.

❦

The next day, awakening from anesthesia, Rich stands at the foot of my bed. *"Baci, baci, baci,"* I say, throwing him kisses, kisses, kisses.

"Si è svegliata. Come sta?" (You're awake. How are you?)

This from the man I hadn't noticed standing bedside. He looks too young to be a doctor but Rich assures me he is. Feeling as though I've had too much to drink, I concentrate on the doctor's moving lips. Unable to focus on the audible, my eyes wander to his name tag. I squint. Too far away to decipher. I reach out and grasp the bottom of his laminated photo I.D. and pull it and, consequently, the doctor, closer to me. When I read his name, Dottore Niccola Bacci, a squeal escapes my lips. The sound of it bounces off the walls, piercing my ears.

Fully conscious now, I hoist myself to a sitting position, slap my knee and blurt to Rich in a high-pitched laugh, "Did you hear that? His name is Dr. Bacci! Can you believe the co-inky-dink?"

Both men take a step backward.

Keeping his distance, Dr. Bacci (pronounced *BAH-chee*) starts over. The surgery had gone well. He repaired my broken tibia near the ankle. The cracked fibula will repair itself without intervention. He says four weeks in a cast. Ah, the cast. The leaden weight of it under the blanket, so new it feels sodden.

I ask Dr. Bacci to raise the head of the bed. He leans over and hand-cranks it to a semi-seated position. I sink back into the pillows, relieved. I've lived through the worst nightmare a traveler dreads – an operation in a foreign hospital. And, unlike the day before, I am pain free, in fact, loopily pain-free.

An aide enters and preps me for moving to another room. Rich and the doctor bid me goodbye as she unhooks the IV bag and places it on the bed. When she lifts the covers at my feet to secure the pillows propped under

169

my leg, I see, for the first time, the plaster-of-Paris cast. It starts below my knee and continues down, encapsulating my foot, except for the toes, which look alarmingly like Miss Piggy's. A tube snakes out of the top of the cast. Following it with my eyes, I lean over the side of the bed – for there are no rail guards – and follow the serpentine plastic to the floor where it empties into an enclosed container collecting a reddish-brown liquid. The aide picks the container up from the floor and also places this on top of the bed.

She pushes me out of the room, into the hallway and onto an elevator so narrow that to join me she has to squish herself between the bed and the compartment's control panel. When we arrive at the correct floor, the doors open, she steps out, audibly exhales and yanks the foot of the bed. She twirls it around and takes me for a breezy ride down the corridor, blasting through several sets of double doors, none of which is automatic. The poor woman constantly juggles pushing and holding doors while keeping the momentum of the bed going and steering it so as not to crash it into door jambs. This lack of automatic doors, I notice, forces people in wheelchairs and on crutches to depend upon the kindness of strangers to navigate through them.

Later I'll learn that this hospital was built only six years ago. Locals consider it to be leap years ahead of the one it replaced. I don't even want to think about the previous one.

The aide sets me up in my new room with a roommate, a heavyset woman with an easy smile. We introduce ourselves. Lidia just had a knee replacement. Unlike many Italians, Lidia speaks slowly so I can semi-understand her.

I've been studying Italian for three years and still have no grace with it. Surprisingly, though, during my stay in the hospital, I manage to speak and understand words I didn't know before and haven't recalled since. I attribute this phenomenon to the enhanced survival mode into which hospital life jettisons nervous people like me.

Left alone, since neither Dr. Bacci nor Rich followed me on my escapade, I notice the massive room Lidia and I share, how the white walls, devoid of decoration, overwhelm a teeny-tiny crucifix hanging below the vaulted ceiling. Adding to the room's spaciousness is the fact that there is only one chair for visitors, no televisions, no telephones, and no privacy curtain to

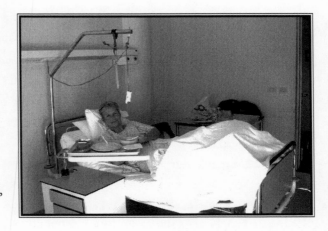

draw between the patients. The only things taking up space are the two beds and two swivel tray tables.

On Lidia's side, floor-to-ceiling windows overlook a stunning panorama of the Apennine Mountains. French doors lead onto a balcony. No screens cover the balcony door or the room's windows which, since it is June, are wide open. When the temperature soars outside, staff roll down the "hurricane" shutters and turn on the air conditioning. Thankfully, the A/C is not kept nearly as cold here as in American hospitals.

In the evening, Rich returns for a visit. "There you are!" he says as he enters. "I've been looking all over for you."

"Did you ask at information?"

"Yeah, but they couldn't find your name."

"How'd you get here then?"

"I asked a doctor where orthopedics was."

"You know the word 'orthopedic' in Italian?"

"I just added an 'o'. *Orthopedico*."

I smile. Sometimes that's all it takes. Other times it doesn't begin to translate.

"Anyway, I've been going up and down this floor for five minutes now, glancing into rooms."

A moment later, Rich's cycling buddy, Giordano, enters. "Ciao,

Giordano!"

He shakes Rich's hand while simultaneously giving him the two-cheeked kiss. Then he leans down and kisses me on each cheek.

I ask him, "Did you have a hard time finding me?" He shakes his head.

"Rich was just saying how difficult it was to find me."

With a slanted grin Giordano says in English, "No, all I do is aska where American woman is."

We all laugh and have a nice visit.

The first night after the operation, I frequently startle awake, each time dreaming I am falling. My hands grasp at air. Before lights-out the second night, I pantomime to an aide what I need. He procures a set of guard rails (apparently stored in a corner of the bathroom I have yet to see), and attach them to my bed.

After the delivery of my first meal, I notice I have no utensils. I catch the attention of my roommate's daughter who races out of the room and chases down the food service aide. When she returns, she hands me a plastic fork, knife and spoon, a victorious smile on her face. It takes me a day and a half to figure out that patients bring, in addition to their own pajamas and toilet paper, their own cutlery and coffee cup.

Patients, such as Lidia, who have a grown daughter living nearby, are the luckiest of all patients. Before each meal, her daughter rushes in, plumps her mother's pillows, cranks up her bed, wets a towel (Europeans do not use washcloths) to wash her hands, arranges her silverware, drapes a poppy-embroidered cloth napkin across her bosom and, once the meal arrives, arranges it on the bed table and swivels it across the bed. She keeps her mother company throughout the meal and, afterward, retrieves dish soap and paper towels from her mother's locker near the entry door. She washes the utensils in the bathroom sink, and then puts them away in a handmade cloth pouch. I look on with envy.

One may question how sanitary it is to wash eating utensils in the bathroom sink, but in the orthopedic ward in Italy, we aren't allowed to get out of bed; bedpans are our exclusive depository. Thus, the bathroom's only purpose is for washing dishes. Oh, and for storing bed rails.

By the end of the second day, Rich has brought me everything I need – toothbrush, soap, and toilet paper (only one roll is given upon admittance), pajamas and robe, brush, comb, lipstick, books to read. Daily, he treats me with a copy of the *Herald-Tribune*, the only English newspaper sold in our town's main square, and a delectable sweet roll and smooth cappuccino from the hospital café.

Friends in the States, who I talk to from my cell phone, scold me for not getting up and moving about right away. "You'll get a clot and die," they warn. (To worry them further, I tell them how no patient wears an I.D. wrist band and no one has identification on or near their bed. I attribute my flippant attitude to the painkillers I'm taking.)

Later in the week, Rich brings me a set of crutches borrowed from our land lady. With him present, I scootch to the edge of the bed. Before I can get my arms into the armholes of the crutches, my roommate and her two visitors scream "No!" in unison. One of them buzzes the nurse so fast you would think I planned to leap off the balcony. I pull myself back into bed. Geez, I think, I didn't really want to get up anyway.

One afternoon Lidia's son comes in carrying a table he'd borrowed from elsewhere in the hospital. With purpose he walks out and when he returns several minutes later, he's lugging a television set. He places it on the table and fiddles with its rabbit ears until the picture comes in fairly well. Apparently an important soccer match will be broadcast that night and Lidia, an ardent fan, wants to watch it.

That evening, the TV seduces a multitude of people (patients and staff, male and female, but mostly male) into our room. If anyone thinks it might be awkward to use a bedpan with no curtain between you and your roommate, imagine what it is like to have strangers standing and sitting around your room all evening when you have to go. I hold it until everyone leaves.

Lidia and I share more than hygiene – we also share the free Italian newspaper delivered daily. We become adept at sliding it across the floor, the distance between the two beds being too great to toss. We lean halfway out of our beds to reel them in close enough to pick up. I need to contort my body since I have guard rails.

Medications come in a plastic saucer which the nurse capsizes into her bare hand and transfers into my hand, or worse, if I'm dozing, dumps them onto my swivel food table which is never washed. I always forget to have someone clean it until the next pill rolls onto it. Then I forget all over again.

The most amazing thing about this hospital is that no one bothers me during the night to take my temperature or blood pressure. It's the first hospital I've been in where I actually sleep. It's also the first hospital I've been in where sleeping pills aren't forced upon me.

At six a.m. a nurse awakens Lidia and me by gently placing a thermometer under one of our arms and taking leave for another ten or fifteen minutes. When she returns, she opens the room to light and collects the thermometers. Soon after, a round-bellied, jolly monk enters and blesses us. His duty done, a nun, who likes to pinch my cheeks, stands in the corridor to lead everyone on the floor in prayer. The petite woman amazes us with how well she can throw her voice.

Breakfast consists of an espresso and pre-packaged toast with a packet of jam. If it were a normal day, this meager fare wouldn't be enough to keep me going until lunchtime. The food served is unremarkable. It's neither good nor bad. But then, food is not as emotional an issue with me as it is with many other people.

Each day, I receive kind, loving care from the doctors, nurses, aides, visitors (mine and Lidia's) and my husband. People wait on me hand and foot. I read and nap and visit. It is a good time. They tell me I will get sprung tomorrow.

As I'm falling asleep, an unwelcome thought creeps out from the recesses of my mind. Something about myself, something that's still out of alignment – besides my leg – has caught up with me and there'll be no escaping it this time. Conventional wisdom says falling down and breaking one's leg is an accident, but deep within me a wiser voice whispers, "There are no accidents." The voice unsettles me. I sense an old wound that's ripe for licking. If I don't face what's been eluding me, I'm sure something far more vital than my leg may break. ♥

27

BACK AT MACRÍ

Once I scrabble out of the car (yes, we broke down and rented one) Rich has parked behind Macrì, I tuck the crutches snugly under my armpits. Heading toward our apartment, my legs swing to and fro, only my left foot touching down. Twenty feet later, I reach the *forno* area and plop into a plastic chair exhausted.

Lucia crosses the lawn, smiling. She bends over to kiss my cheeks and welcomes me home. She says something to Rich and me in Italian. Looking up at her, I shade my eyes. I can't imagine what she said. She repeats the sentence, turning her hand first one way and then the other.

Together, Rich and I figure it out. She said, "It's a good thing you broke your leg this way instead of that way or they wouldn't have been able to put the rod in."

What rod? I didn't know they put a rod in. I turn sideways in the chair, rest my arm over its back and ask, "If you don't mind my asking, how do *you* know?"

She answers in an offhanded manner. "My friend is a nurse and she was in the operating room with you."

Say, *what*! I look down at the heavy plaster cast, trying to imagine what my leg looked like in the operating room. Then I chuckle, wondering if she saw me drooling too. So much for privacy! Small-town living, that's what this is.

After a few niceties, Lucia goes back to work while I continue hobbling my way into the entryway of our apartment. Sitting on the bottom step, I hand the crutches to Rich and lift myself onto the next step with my arms behind me, palms pressing into the stone. By the time I reach the top, my triceps burn.

For days I laze around with my foot propped up. People visit. They sign the cast. Quinto decides to sign it on behalf of his dog, "Deke." Only he spells it "Dick." Of course! I nearly knock myself out slapping my forehead. If the car rental company Avis is pronounced "Ah-vees" by Italians, ergo, "Dick" becomes "Deke." The "i" is a long "eee" sound in Italian. It seems no matter how long I live and how much I learn I'm continually surprised.

During my recuperation, Rich does all the grocery shopping, cooking and cleaning. Having little to do, I develop an abscessed tooth (yes, again!), and Rich brings me back to Dr. Pierone. When the dentist sees me on crutches, he shakes his head. I think he thinks I'm a basket case. I think he's right.

Another one hundred euros for a well-executed root canal. I'm thinking I should always come to Italy for my dental work. The savings alone would pay for my plane ticket!

July Fourth – not an Italian holiday – arrives. I'm sitting in the hot apartment with my leg propped on a chair. A fan blows directly on me. I'm in what I call "imposed couch time." Rich is riding bikes with Giordano. He made my breakfast and lunch before he took off, and he'll return in time to make dinner. It's not a bad life, except for the thinking.

I examine how I feel about Rich biking his buns off while mine are spreading out on the couch like pancake batter. There was a time when this would've made me feel left out and left behind. Not anymore. Over the years, thanks to menstrual cramps, giving birth, surgeries (several on my feet) and bouts of depression, I've made friends with the couch. That friendship doesn't make it any less painful, but at least now it doesn't frustrate me anymore.

Between the root canal (which I take to mean a root belief of mine is faulty) and the broken leg (which I take to mean that something is fractured), I pray the same prayer I prayed to quit smoking. Once again, I ask the universe for the *willingness* to discover the problem. Then I let go and trust.

I pick up a book and start reading. After a few chapters a character in the book says, "Yes, she always wants people to think her dog is bigger than yours." This time the universe answers so quickly I almost miss the portal. I lay the book in my lap and stare out the window, the purple Apennines standing strong and silent in the distance.

I get to wondering why I've always felt so competitive with Rich. It's particularly strange since he never wanted to play that game. Oh, he went along with it on our honeymoon in the Ozarks, when I'd challenge, really *challenge*, him to a game of miniature golf. While he competed for fun, I competed to try to show him I was better. Of course that never turned out as I'd hoped, for he always won. Good thing he knew enough not to throw a game. The ramifications would have been too severe.

Sitting on the couch now, I realize it's not important where that egocentric drive to win came from so much as how funny it seems now. I mean, really … miniature golf? And I think Momar Qaddafi is an egomaniac?

I'm old enough now to know that I can change in an instant. What takes so long is deciding to change, to become *willing* to change.

Tomorrow I get this cast cut off and the stitches taken out. I can't wait to scratch what must be a very hairy leg. We'll need to go to a medical supply store afterward to buy a walking cast, even though I won't be able to put an ounce of weight on my foot for months to come.

We're flying back to the States in a few days. I'm ready. Matt and Hai Yan are living in our house now, and they're about to make us grandparents for the first time. There's a lot to look forward to. There's a lot to be grateful for. And there's a lot more to learn. The footpath never ends.

ACKNOWLEDGMENTS

The myriad ways people help, support and assist in the creation of a manuscript would comprise a book in itself. This one is no exception.

Although I've tried to remember everyone, please accept my apologies in advance if I did not give credit where credit is due.

First, to the kind and generous people in Italy: Giuseppe Nardi, Nerina Zen, Quinto Curzio, Liana Curzio, Giordano Castagnoli, Clemenza Maria Milianti, Lucia Vinagli-Macrì, Maria Giuseppina Macrì, Maria Teresa Boriosi Vinagli, Roberta Marsili, Luigi Brenvaldi, Nadia Murarotto, Dr. Pierpaolo Pieroni, Dr. Niccola Bacci, Sandro Belletti, Sandro Galvani, Tullio Pavanelli, Andrea Capanni, Vallì Tarzaria, Francesco Tavernelli, and Zafer Iqbal Gondal.

To my writers' group: Margie Reins Smith, Wilma Montle, Marlene Mayer Harle, Dianne Peters Pegg, and a special thanks to Phyllis Reeve. I've lost count as to how many times Phyllis has read the manuscript. However, it should be noted that additions and deletions were made after her last edit, so any errors are mine and mine alone.

To the following people who supported my efforts in a myriad of ways: Sara Reeside, Lisa Mower Gandelot, Daphne Harrie, Carol C. Godwin, Nancy Thomas, Suzanne Ross, Mary Minock, Jean Kroll, Patricia Steele, Peter Clifford, Marsha Clifford, Jenni Prestininzi, Vince Bonasso, Fausta Bonasso, Katie Elsila and Laney Corrado.

Last, and certainly not least, thank you to my husband, Rich. Never in a million years would I have ever attempted an adventure this far from home without him. I will always feel grateful for his unwavering support of all the paths I've pursued over the years, both internal and external.